# THE ANATOMY OF PEACE

**Leadership and Self-Deception**
Getting Out of the Box
*Third Edition*


**The Outward Mindset**
How to Change Lives and Transform Organizations
*Second Edition*

# THE ANATOMY OF PEACE

RESOLVING THE HEART OF CONFLICT

*Revised and Expanded Fourth Edition*

THE ARBINGER INSTITUTE

BK

Berrett–Koehler Publishers, Inc.

This edition is published in arrangement with Berrett-Koehler Publishers, Inc.

Berrett-Koehler Publishers, Inc.
1333 Broadway, Suite 1000
Oakland, CA 94612-1921
Tel: (510) 817-2277
Fax: (510) 817-2278
www.bkconnection.com

Ordering Information

**Quantity sales.** Special discounts are available on quantity purchases by corporations, associations, and others. For details, contact the "Special Sales Department" at the Berrett-Koehler address above.

**Individual sales.** Berrett-Koehler publications are available through most bookstores. They can also be ordered directly from Berrett-Koehler: Tel: (800) 929-2929; Fax: (802) 864-7626; www.bkconnection.com.

**Orders for college textbook/course adoption use.** Please contact Berrett-Koehler: Tel: (800) 929-2929; Fax: (802) 864-7626.

Distributed to the U.S. trade and internationally by Penguin Random House Publisher Services.

Berrett-Koehler and the BK logo are registered trademarks of Berrett-Koehler Publishers, Inc.

Printed in the United States of America

Berrett-Koehler books are printed on long-lasting acid-free paper. When it is available, we choose paper that has been manufactured by environmentally responsible processes. These may include using trees grown in sustainable forests, incorporating recycled paper, minimizing chlorine in bleaching, or recycling the energy produced at the paper mill.

Library of Congress Cataloging-in-Publication Data

Names: Arbinger Institute, issuer.
Title: The anatomy of peace : resolving the heart of conflict / The
  Arbinger Institute.
Description: Revised and Expanded Fourth Edition. | Oakland, CA :
  Berrett-Koehler, [2022] | Revised edition of The anatomy of peace,
  [2020] | Includes bibliographical references and index.
Identifiers: LCCN 2021034192 (print) | LCCN 2021034193 (ebook) | ISBN
  9781523001132 (paperback) | ISBN 9781523001149 (adobe pdf) | ISBN
  9781523001156 (epub)
Subjects: LCSH: Conflict management. | Interpersonal conflict. |
  Peace—Psychological aspects.
Classification: LCC HM1126 .A53 2022  (print) | LCC HM1126  (ebook) | DDC
  303.6/9—dc23
LC record available at https://lccn.loc.gov/2021034192
LC ebook record available at https://lccn.loc.gov/2021034193

Fourth Edition
29 28 27 26 25 24 23 22    10 9 8 7 6 5 4 3 2

Copyedit and proofreading: PeopleSpeak
Cover and book design and composition: Michael Brown

"Our fate is shaped from within ourselves outward, never from without inward."

**JACQUES LUSSEYRAN**

# CONTENTS

**PART IV  SPREADING PEACE**

RESOURCES FOR READERS
**APPLYING *THE ANATOMY OF PEACE* TO DIVERSITY, EQUITY, INCLUSION & BELONGING**

## NOTE TO READERS

Although many of the stories in this book were inspired by actual events, no character or organization described in this book represents any specific person or organization. This is a work of fiction—a story to help each of us see and understand the truth that may be hidden in our own story.

# PREFACE

The world is in turmoil. Our homes, our workplaces, our communities, and certainly our politics are riddled with strife. Conflict is ubiquitous. Political differences, rampant racism, divisive phobias, gender-based discrimination, religious bigotry, ethnic divides, and other prejudices and intolerance of every kind threaten family relationships, fuel conflicts within communities and between nations, and undermine organizational performance. These challenges are not new, but the strains on interpersonal and societal relationships in all directions seem to be increasing. In this day and age, perhaps nothing is more important than knowing how to heal our deepest divides and maintain connection when people are pulling apart.

Corporate leaders recognize both the challenge and the need. The 2013 *Executive Coaching Survey* published by Stanford University reveals that CEOs feel a greater need to improve their conflict management skills than skills of any other type. Partners who are struggling with each other and parents who feel challenged by their children undoubtedly identify the same need. Furthermore, people in countries the world over yearn for governmental leaders who know how to find ways to work more effectively with rivals for the good of their countries.

Which raises this question: why is there so much confusion regarding how to deal with conflict when there is so much need?

The answer is that when parties are in conflict, they actually don't want what they think they want. We assume that people in conflict want solutions, but the truth is that more often than not they unwittingly work against their own objectives. Parents of belligerent children do want the belligerence to end, those who work for tyrannical managers want an end to the tyranny, and citizens of vulnerable nations certainly want to be treated with respect. Notice, however, that parties in conflict all wait on the same solution: they wait for the other party to change. Should we be surprised, then, when conflicts linger and problems remain?

It turns out that people in conflict too often value something else more highly than they value solutions. *The Anatomy of Peace* shows what this is and demonstrates how conflicts at home, conflicts at work, and conflicts in the world stem from the same root cause. The book shows how we systematically misunderstand that cause and unwittingly perpetuate the very problems we think we are trying to solve. Most importantly, it presents proven methodologies for bringing people together and resolving conflicts in fundamental and lasting ways.

*The Anatomy of Peace* has been instrumental in overcoming inequity, conflict, and cultural dysfunction of all kinds in organizations. Its ideas have been successfully implemented to transform law enforcement methodologies and results, heal labor-management rifts, reinvent nonprofit initiatives, reimagine corporate cultures, and heal communities. Business and governmental leaders, parents, professors, and conflict professionals alike use the book as a guide for finding solutions to their most challenging problems.

This fourth edition includes revisions throughout the book to increase its relevance and usefulness at a time of deeply entrenched conflict throughout society and an urgent need to combat racism and prejudice in their many manifestations. Additionally, this edition includes new detailed discussions that illuminate the origin of bias and the pattern of dehumanization that lies at the heart of today's most pressing societal and organizational challenges—challenges that cannot be solved until the origins of the bias and discrimination, evidenced in racism, sexism, ableism, homophobia, religious bigotry, and divisive othering of all kinds, are properly understood and addressed. To assist in the practical application of these concepts to increase diversity, equity, and inclusion in organizations, we have included a practical guide in the "Resources for Readers" section at the end of this book.

Since it was first published in 2006, *The Anatomy of Peace* has been printed in over thirty languages and has become a perennial bestseller in the conflict resolution space. Year after year, *The Anatomy of Peace* has been one of the top-selling conflict resolution books in the world. Few books have performed so strongly in their categories over such a long time.

We author our books as an institute because, as a global organization dedicated to sharing these ideas with the world, many individuals collaborate to develop these ideas together. Furthermore, we stand on the shoulders of many who founded the institute and pioneered the development of the concepts you will read about in these pages.

The book itself unfolds as a story. While the historical and contemporary conflicts that form the backdrop of the story are very

real, all of the characters in the book and Camp Moriah itself—
the setting where the book unfolds—are completely fictional. The
characters of Yusuf al-Falah, an Arab, and Avi Rozen, a Jew, each
lost his father at the hands of the other's ethnic cousins.

*The Anatomy of Peace* is the story of how they came together,
how they help others come together, and how we too can find our
way out of the struggles that weigh us down.

Those who have read our earlier book, *Leadership and Self-
Deception,* will recognize one of the key characters from that book,
Lou Herbert, as *The Anatomy of Peace* takes the reader back in time
to when Lou and his wife, Carol, first learned the ideas that transformed both Lou's company and their family.

In many respects, the characters portrayed in this book are each
of us. They share our strengths and our weaknesses, our aspirations and our despair. They are seeking solutions to problems that
weigh us down. They are us, and we are them. So their lessons offer
us hope.

Hope? Yes. Because our problems, as theirs, are not what they
seem. This is at once our challenge and our opportunity.

# THE ANATOMY OF PEACE

## PART I

# THE HEART OF PEACE

# 1 • ENEMIES IN THE DESERT

"I'm not going!" The teenage girl's shriek pulled everyone's attention to her. "You can't make me go!"

The woman she was yelling at attempted to sound calm. "Jenny, listen to me."

"I'm not going! I don't care what you say. I won't!"

At this, the girl turned and faced a middle-aged man who seemed torn between taking her into his arms and slinking away unnoticed. "Daddy, please!" The girl broke into sobs.

Lou Herbert, who was watching the scene from across the parking lot, knew before Jenny spoke that this was her father. He could see himself in the man. He recognized the ambivalence he felt toward his own child, eighteen-year-old Cory, who was standing stiffly at his side.

Cory had recently spent a year in prison for a drug conviction. Less than three months after his release, he was arrested for stealing $1,000 worth of prescription painkillers, bringing more shame upon himself and, Lou thought, the family. Lou didn't like the idea of needing help with personal family matters, but things had gotten out of hand. This was a last resort.

He looked back at Jenny and her father, whom she was now clutching in desperation. Lou was glad Cory had been sent here by court order. It meant that a stunt like Jenny's would earn Cory another stint in jail. Lou was pretty sure their morning would pass without incident.

"Lou, over here."

Carol, Lou's wife, was motioning for him to join her. He tugged at Cory's arm. "Come on, your mom wants us."

"Lou, this is Yusuf al-Falah," she said, introducing the man standing next to her. "Mr. al-Falah's the one who's been helping us get everything arranged for Cory."

"Of course," Lou said, forcing a smile.

Yusuf al-Falah was the Arab half of an odd partnership in the Arizona desert. An immigrant from Jerusalem, he came to the United States in the 1960s to further his education and ended up staying, eventually becoming a professor of education at Arizona State University. In the summer of 1978, he befriended a young and bitter Israeli man, Avi Rozen, who had come to the States following the death of his father in the Yom Kippur War of 1973. At the time, Avi was flunking out of school. In an experimental program, he and others struggling with their grades were given a chance to rehabilitate their college careers and transcripts during a long summer in the high mountains and deserts of Arizona. Al-Falah, Rozen's elder by fifteen years, led the program.

It was a forty-day course in survival, the kind of experience Arabs and Israelis of al-Falah and Rozen's era had been steeped in from their youth. Over those forty days, the two men made a connection. Muslim and Jewish, both regarded land—sometimes the very same land—as sacred. Out of this shared respect for the soil gradually grew a respect for each other, despite their differences in belief and the strife that divided their people.

Or so Lou had been told.

In truth, Lou was skeptical of the happy face that had been

painted on the relationship between al-Falah and Rozen. To him it smelled like PR, a game Lou knew from his own corporate market-ing experience. *Come be healed by two former enemies who now raise their families together in peace.* The more he thought about the al-Falah/Rozen story, the less he believed it.

If he had examined himself at that moment, Lou would have been forced to admit that it was precisely this Middle Eastern intrigue surrounding Camp Moriah, as it was called, that had lured him onto the plane with Carol and Cory. Certainly he had every reason not to come. Five executives had recently left his company, putting the organization in peril. If he had to spend two days away, which al-Falah and Rozen were requiring, he needed to unwind on a golf course or near a pool, not commiserate with a group of despairing parents.

"Thank you for helping us," he said to al-Falah, feigning grati-tude. He continued watching the girl out of the corner of his eye. She was still shrieking between sobs and clinging to her father like a cat on a tree trunk. "Looks like you have your hands full here."

Al-Falah's eyes creased in a smile. "I suppose we do. Parents can become a bit hysterical on occasions like this."

*Parents?* Lou thought. *The girl is the one in hysterics.* But al-Falah had struck up a conversation with Cory before Lou could correct him.

"You must be Cory."

"That would be me," Cory said flippantly.

Lou registered his disapproval by digging his fingers into Cory's biceps.

Cory flexed in response.

"I'm glad to meet you," al-Falah said, taking no notice of Cory's tone. "I've been looking forward to it." Leaning in, he added, "No doubt more than you have. I can't imagine you're very excited to be here."

Cory hesitated. "Not really. No," he finally said, yanking his arm out of his father's grasp. He reflexively brushed his bicep, as if to dust off any molecular vestige that might have remained from his father's grip.

"Don't blame you." Al-Falah looked at Lou and then back at Cory. "Don't blame you a bit. But you know something?"

Cory looked at him warily.

"I'd be surprised if you feel that way for long. You might. But I'd be surprised." He patted Cory on the back. "I'm just glad you're here, Cory."

"Yeah, okay. Whatever you say."

Lou shot Cory an angry look.

"So, Lou," al-Falah said, "you're probably not too excited about being here either, are you?"

"On the contrary." Lou forced a smile. "We're quite happy to be here."

Carol, standing beside him, knew that wasn't at all true. But he did come. She had to give him that. He often complained about inconveniences, but in the end he most often made the inconvenient choice when it came to Cory's well-being. She reminded herself to stay focused on this positive fact—on the good that lay not too far beneath the surface.

"We're glad you're here, Lou." Turning to Carol, al-Falah added, "We know what it means for a mother to leave her child in the hands of another. It is an honor that you would give us the privilege."

"Thank you, Mr. al-Falah. It means a lot to hear you say that," Carol said.

"Well, it's how we feel," he responded. "And please, call me Yusuf. You too, Cory." He turned in Cory's direction. "In fact, especially you. Please call me Yusuf. Or 'Yusi,' if you want. That's what most of the young people call me."

In place of the self-righteous sarcasm he had exhibited so far, Cory simply nodded.

A few minutes later, Carol and Lou watched as Cory loaded into a van with the others who would be spending the next sixty days in the wilderness. All, that is, except for the girl Jenny, who, when she realized her father wouldn't be rescuing her, ran across the street and sat belligerently on a short concrete wall. Lou noticed she wasn't wearing anything on her feet. He looked skyward at the rising Arizona sun. *She'll have some sense burned into her before long,* he thought.

Jenny's parents seemed lost as to what to do. Lou saw Yusuf go over to them, and a couple of minutes later the parents went into the building, glancing back one last time at their daughter. Jenny howled as they stepped through the doors and out of her sight.

Lou and Carol milled about the parking lot with a few of the other parents, engaging in small talk. They visited with a woman named Gwyn Murray and her husband, Pettis, from Dallas, Texas; Miguel and Ria Lopez from Corvallis, Oregon; and a woman named Elizabeth Wingfield from London, England. Mrs. Wingfield was currently living in Berkeley, California, where her husband was a visiting professor in Middle Eastern studies. Like Lou, her attraction to Camp Moriah was mostly due to her curiosity about the founders and their history. She was only reluctantly accompanying her nephew, whose parents couldn't afford the trip from England.

Carol made a remark about it being a geographically diverse group except for Jenny's parents, Teri and Carl, who lived in Phoenix. Though everyone nodded and smiled, it was obvious that these conversations were barely registering. Most of the parents were preoccupied with their kids in the van and cast furtive glances in their direction every minute or so. If trudging through the desert worked, at what cost? How many of these kids would never forgive their guardians? For Lou's part, he was most interested in why nobody seemed to be doing anything about Jenny.

Lou was about to ask Yusuf what he was going to do so that the vehicle could set out to take their children to the trail. Just then, however, Yusuf patted the man he was talking to on the back and began to walk toward the street. Jenny didn't acknowledge him.

"Jenny," he called out to her. "Are you all right?"

"What do you think?" she shrieked back. "You can't make me go. You can't!"

"You're right, Jenny, we can't. And we wouldn't. Whether you go will be up to you."

Lou turned to the van, hoping Cory hadn't heard this. *Maybe you can't make him go, Yusi,* he thought, *but I can. And so can the court.*

Yusuf didn't say anything. He just stood there, looking across the street at the girl while cars occasionally passed between them. "Would you mind if I came over, Jenny?" he finally called.

She didn't say anything.

"I'll just come over and we can talk."

Yusuf crossed the street and sat down on the sidewalk. Lou strained to hear what they were saying but couldn't for the distance and traffic.

"Okay, everyone, it's about time to get started."

Lou turned toward the voice. A short youngish-looking man stood at the doorway to the building, beaming with what Lou thought was an overdone smile. He had a thick head of hair that made him look younger than he was. "Come on in, if you would," he said. "We should probably be getting started."

"What about our kids?" Lou pointed at the idling vehicle.

"They'll be leaving shortly, I'm sure," the man responded. "You've had a chance to say good-bye, haven't you?"

They all nodded.

"Good. Then this way, please."

Lou took a last look at the vehicle. Cory was staring straight ahead, apparently paying no attention to them. Carol was crying and waving at him anyway as the parents shuffled through the door.

"Avi Rozen," said the bushy-haired man as he extended his hand to Lou.

"Lou and Carol Herbert," Lou replied in the perfunctory tone he used with those who worked for him.

"Pleasure to meet you, Lou. Welcome, Carol," Avi said with an encouraging nod. They filed through the door with the others and went up the stairs. This was to be their home for the next two days. *Two days during which we'd better learn what they're going to do to fix our son,* Lou thought.

# 2 • DEEPER MATTERS

Lou looked around the room. Ten or so chairs were arranged in a semicircle. *This is going to get awkward,* he thought. Lou sat in the first chair, on the outside edge of the semicircle. Jenny's father and mother were sitting across from him. The mother's face was drawn tight with worry. Blotchy red patches covered the skin on her neck and stretched across her face. The father was staring vacantly at the ground.

Behind them, Elizabeth Wingfield—*a bit overdressed,* Lou thought, in a chic business suit—was helping herself to a cup of tea at the bar against the far wall of the room.

Meanwhile, Gwyn and Pettis Murray, the couple from Dallas, were taking their seats about halfway around the semicircle to Lou's right. Gwyn seemed pretty sharp to Lou, and Pettis carried himself with the air of an executive—head high, jaw set, guarded.

On the other side of Gwyn and Pettis sat Miguel Lopez, a hulk of a man with massive arms. He wore a beard and mustache so full that a black bandana tied tightly around his forehead was the only thing that kept his face from being completely obscured by hair. By contrast, his wife, Ria, was barely over five feet tall. In the parking lot, she had been the most talkative of the group, while Miguel had mostly stood by in silence. Ria now nodded at Carol and Lou, the corners of her mouth hinting at a smile. Lou tipped his head toward her in acknowledgment and then continued scanning the room.

Lou turned to the front of the room, arms folded loosely across his chest. One thing he hated was wasting time, and it seemed they had been doing nothing but that since they'd arrived. Even worse, the seating arrangement told him they were going to be asked to share their feelings—a painful waste of time and energy.

"Thank you all for coming," Avi said as he walked to the front. "I've been looking forward to meeting you in person and to getting to know your children. First of all, I know you're concerned about them—Teri and Carl, you especially," he said, glancing for a moment over at Jenny's parents. "Your presence here is a testament to your love for your children. You needn't trouble yourself about them. They will be well taken care of."

"In fact," he said after a brief pause, "they are not my primary concern."

"Who is, then?" Ria asked.

"You are, Ria. All of you."

"We are?" Lou repeated in surprise.

"Yes," Avi smiled.

Lou was never one to back down from a perceived challenge. In Vietnam he had served as a sergeant in the Marine Corps, and the gruesome experience had both hardened and sharpened him. His men referred to him as Hellfire Herbert, a name that reflected both his loud, brash nature and his consequences-be-damned devotion to his unit. His men both feared and revered him: for most of them, he was the last person on earth they would want to spend a holiday with, but no other leader in the Marines brought more men back alive.

"And why are we your primary concern?" Lou asked.

"Because you don't think you should be."

Lou laughed politely. "That's a bit circular, isn't it?"

The others in the group, like spectators at a tennis match, looked back at Avi, anticipating his reply.

Avi smiled and looked down at the ground for a moment, thinking. "Tell us about Cory, Lou," he said finally. "What's he like?"

"Cory?" Lou said.

"Yes."

"He is a boy with great potential who is wasting his life," Lou answered matter-of-factly.

"But he's a wonderful boy," Carol interjected, glancing warily at Lou. "He's made some mistakes, but he's basically a good kid."

"'Good kid'?" Lou scoffed, losing his air of nonchalance. "He's a *felon* for heaven's sake—twice over! Sure he has the ability to be good, but mere potential doesn't make him good. We wouldn't be here if he was such a good kid."

Carol bit her lip, and the other parents in the room fidgeted uncomfortably.

Sensing the discomfort around him, Lou leaned forward and added, "Sorry to speak so plainly, but I'm not here to celebrate my child's meager achievements. Frankly, I'm really angry with my son."

"Lou is quite right," Avi said now turning to the group. "We are here not because our children have been choosing well but because they have been choosing poorly."

"That's what I'm saying," Lou said.

Avi smiled. "So what, then, is the solution? How can the problems you are experiencing in your families be improved?"

"I should think that's obvious." Lou leaned back. "We are here because our children have problems. And Camp Moriah is in the business of helping children overcome their problems. Isn't that right?"

Carol bristled at Lou's tone. He was now speaking in his board-room voice—direct, challenging, and abrasive. He rarely took this tone with her, but it had become the voice of his interactions with Cory over the last few years. Carol couldn't remember the last time Lou and Cory had an actual conversation. When they spoke, it was a kind of verbal wrestling match, each of them trying to antici-pate the other's moves, searching for weaknesses they could then exploit to force the other into submission. With no actual mat into which to press the other, these verbal matches always ended in a draw: each of them claimed hollow victory while living with ongo-ing defeat. She silently called heavenward for help, as she had been taught to do by her churchgoing parents. She wasn't sure there was a heaven or any help to be had, but she broadcast her need all the same.

Avi smiled good-naturedly. "So, Lou," he said, "Cory is a prob-lem. That's what you're saying."

"Yes."

"He needs to be fixed in some way—changed, motivated, disci-plined, corrected." Avi waited for a reply.

"Absolutely," Lou said.

"And you've tried that?"

"Tried what?"

"Changing him."

"Of course."

"And has it worked?" Avi asked. "Has he changed?"

"Not yet," Lou said. "But that's why we're here. One day, no matter how hard a skull he has, he's going to get it. One way or the other."

"Maybe," Avi said.

"You don't think your program will work?" Lou asked.

"That depends."

"On what?"

"On you." Avi waited for the inevitable pushback.

Lou grunted. "How can the success of your program depend on me when you're the ones who will be working with my son over the coming two months?"

"Because you will be living with him over all the months afterward," Avi answered. "We can help, but if your family environment is the same when he gets home as it was when he left, whatever good happens here is unlikely to make much of a difference later. Yusuf and I are only temporary surrogates. You and Carol, all of you with your respective children," he said, motioning to the group, "are the helpers who matter."

*Great,* Lou thought. *A waste of time.*

"You said you want Cory to change," came a voice from the back, yanking Lou from his thoughts. It was Yusuf, who had finally joined the group.

"Affirmative," Lou said.

"I don't blame you," Yusuf said. "But if that is what you want, there is something you need to know."

"What's that?"

"If you are going to invite change in him, there is something that first must change in you."

"Oh yeah? And what would that be?"

Yusuf walked to the whiteboard that covered nearly the entire front wall of the room. "Let me draw something for you," he said.

## THE INFLUENCE PYRAMID

"By the end of the day tomorrow," Yusuf said, turning to face the group, "we will have formulated a detailed strategy for helping others to change. That strategy will be guided by a diagram we call the Influence Pyramid. We aren't yet ready to consider the pyramid in detail, so I've drawn only its basic structure. This overall structure will help us to discover a fundamental change that must occur in *us* if we are going to invite change in *others*."

"Okay, I'll bite," Lou said. "*What* fundamental change?"

"Look at the two areas in the pyramid," Yusuf said. "Notice that the largest area by far is what I have labeled 'Helping things go right.' In comparison, the 'Dealing with things that are going wrong' area is tiny."

"Okay," Lou said, wondering what significance this had.

"The pyramid," Yusuf continued, "suggests that we should spend much more time and effort helping things go right than dealing with things that are going wrong. Unfortunately, however, these allocations of time and effort are typically reversed. We spend most of our time with others dealing with things that are going wrong. We try fixing our children, changing our spouses, correcting our employees, and disciplining those who aren't acting as we'd like. And when we're not actually *doing* these things, we're *thinking* about doing them or *worrying* about doing them. Am I right?" Yusuf looked around the room for a response.

"For example, Lou," he said, "would it be fair to say that you spend much of your time with Cory criticizing and challenging him?"

There was some truth to this, but Lou didn't want to admit to it so easily.

"Yes, I'd say that's true," Carol admitted for him.

"Thanks," Lou mumbled under his breath.

Carol looked straight ahead.

"It's certainly far too true of me as well," Yusuf said, coming to Lou's rescue. "It's only natural when confronting a problem that we try to correct it. Trouble is, when working with people, this hardly ever helps. Further correction rarely helps a child who is pouting, for example, or a spouse who is brooding or a coworker who is blaming. In other words, most problems in life are not solved merely by correction."

"So what do you suggest?" Lou said. "If your child was into drugs, what would you do, Yusuf? Just ignore it? Are you saying I shouldn't try to change him?"

"Maybe," Yusuf said, "we should begin with a less extreme situation."

"Less extreme?" Lou said, his voice rising in anger. "This is my life! That's what I'm dealing with."

"Yes," Yusuf said, "but it's not all that you are dealing with. You and Carol aren't on drugs, but I bet that doesn't mean you're always happy together."

Lou thought back to the silent treatment Carol had given him on the flight the day before. She didn't like how he had handled Cory, and she communicated her displeasure by clamming up. Tears often lay just below the surface of her silence. Lou knew what her silence meant—that he, Lou, wasn't measuring up—and he resented it. He was having enough trouble with his boy; he didn't think he deserved the pitiful, teary lectures. "It's not easy living with a drug addict. We're not perfect," Lou said.

"Nor am I with my wife, Lina," Yusuf said. "And you know what I've found? When Lina is upset with me in some way, the least helpful thing I can do is criticize her or try to correct her. When she's mad, she has her reasons. I might think she's wrong and her reasons illegitimate, but I've never once convinced her of that by fighting back." He looked at Lou and Carol. "How about you? Has criticism helped you change each other?"

Lou chewed tentatively on the inside of his cheek as he remembered fights he and Carol had gotten into over his critiques and her silent treatment. "No, I suppose not. Not generally, anyway."

"So," Yusuf said, "for many problems in life, solutions will have to be deeper than strategies of discipline or correction."

Lou thought about that for a moment.

"But now for your harder question," Yusuf continued. "What if my child is doing something really harmful, like drugs? What then? Shouldn't I try to change him?"

"Exactly," Lou nodded.

"And the answer to that, of course," Yusuf said, "is yes."

This caught Lou by surprise, and he swallowed the retort he'd been planning.

"But," Yusuf said, "I won't invite my child to change if my interactions with him are primarily in order to get him to change."

Lou got lost in that answer. He began to reload his objection.

"I become an agent of change," Yusuf continued, "only to the degree that I begin to live to help things go right rather than simply to correct things that are going wrong. Rather than simply correcting, for example, I need to reenergize my teaching, my helping, my listening, my learning. I need to put time and effort into building relationships. In other words, if I don't work the bottom part of the pyramid, I won't be successful at the top. Jenny, for example, is currently outside on a wall, refusing to join the others on the trail."

*Still?* Lou thought to himself.

"She doesn't want to enter the program. That's understandable, really. What seventeen-year-old young woman is dying to spend sixty days sleeping on the hard ground and living on cornmeal and critters they can capture with homemade spears?"

"That's what they have to do out there?" Ria asked.

"Well, kind of." Yusuf smiled. "It's not quite that primitive."

"But it's close," Avi interjected with a chuckle.

Ria widened her eyes and rocked backward into her seat, trying to imagine how her boy would do in this environment. By contrast, her husband, Miguel, nodded approvingly.

"So what do we do?" Yusuf asked rhetorically. "Any attempt to discipline or to correct her behavior is unlikely to work, wouldn't you agree?"

"Oh, I don't know," Lou said, arguing more out of habit now than conviction. "If it were me, I would have gone over to her and told her to get her backside into the vehicle."

"And what if she had refused?" Yusuf asked.

"Then I would have made her go," Lou shot back.

"But Camp Moriah is a private organization with no authority of the state," Yusuf said. "We have no desire to create additional problems by trying to bully people into doing what we want them to do. We do not force children to enroll."

"Then you have a problem," Lou said.

"Yes, we certainly do," Yusuf agreed. "The same problem we each have in our families. And the same problem coworkers and countries have with one another. We are all surrounded by other autonomous people who don't always behave as we'd like."

"So what can you do when that's the case?" Ria asked.

"Get really good at the deeper matters," Yusuf said, "at helping things to go right."

Ria frowned. "And how do you get good at that?"

"That is exactly what we are here to talk about for the next two days." Yusuf looked around the room at the group. "Let's begin with the deepest matter of all, an issue I would like to introduce by going back 900 years to something that occurred in the part of the world where Avi and I come from."

Lou rolled his eyes.

# 3 • PEACE IN WARTIME

"In June of 1099," Yusuf began, "Crusaders from the West laid siege to Jerusalem. After forty days, they penetrated the northern wall and flooded into the city. They slaughtered most of the city's Muslim population within two days. The last of the survivors were forced to carry the dead to mass unmarked graves, where they piled the corpses in heaps and set them on fire. These survivors were then either massacred or sold into slavery."

Lou wondered what any of this had to do with his son's behavior issues.

"The Jews," Yusuf continued, "although not so numerous, fared no better. In the Jewish quarter, the inhabitants fled to the main synagogue for refuge. The invaders barricaded the exits and stacked wood around the building. They then torched it, burning all but the few who managed to escape. These people were slaughtered in the narrow streets as they attempted to flee."

About half of the group was engaged. Others, like Lou, wondered where this was going.

"The brutality extended as well to the local Christians who officiated at Christian holy sites. These priests were expelled, tortured, and forced to disclose the location of precious relics, which were then taken from them." Yusuf paused to gather his thoughts.

"This was the beginning of nearly two centuries of strife between invaders from the West and the people of the Middle East. In the minds of many in the Middle East, today's battles are a continuation of this ancient battle for the Holy Land. They view American and European powers as crusading invaders.

"But I think it's important to understand the history of Jerusalem. It was Jewish through most of ancient times until Rome sacked it in 70 AD. After the death of Christ, believers began to spread his teachings through the region. Christianity eventually became the official faith of the Roman Empire and quickly spread through all its territories, including Jerusalem. By 638 AD, the year Muslims captured Jerusalem, it had been a fully Christian city for 300 years. So when the knights of the First Crusade took Jerusalem, in their minds they were retaking what had been taken from them. Like the Muslims they were fighting, they believed the city was rightfully theirs."

"That doesn't justify the atrocities, though," Pettis interjected.

"No," Elizabeth agreed, "it doesn't."

"Oh, come on," Lou said, "the Crusaders didn't have a monopoly on atrocity. The Muslims' hands were dirty too."

"Lou is right about that," Elizabeth said. "There is ugliness on all sides of this conflict. I know a little of this history—I used to teach history to secondary school students. Yusuf gave an example of atrocities by Westerners. But an early Muslim example would be the massacre of the Banu Qurayza, the last Jewish tribe in Medina. In the earliest days of Islam, Muslim armies beheaded the entire tribe."

"And today they blow themselves up in order to maim and murder innocent civilians," Lou blurted.

Elizabeth's mouth stretched disapprovingly into a line. She

hated how an entire religious population could be so casually grouped and defined by the actions of a relative few.

"You certainly know your history, Elizabeth," Yusuf said. "And I agree with you that there are sordid details on all sides of this history. What we would like to introduce all of you to, however, is one not-so-sordid figure."

Lou braced himself for another lecture.

"After taking Jerusalem in 1099, the Crusaders took control of most of the coastal areas of the Middle East. They continued to hold these regions for about eighty years. They succeeded largely because of infighting between rival Muslim military and political leaders. This began to change, however, with the rise to power of the Turkish sultan Nûr al-Dîn, who unified the various peoples of Syria. The tide turned entirely in favor of the Muslim resistance under his successor, Yûsuf Salâh al-Dîn, or simply 'Saladin,' as he is known in the West. Saladin united all the Muslim peoples from Syria to Egypt and mobilized their collective resistance. His armies recaptured Jerusalem in 1187."

Elizabeth nodded in the affirmative.

Yusuf continued: "Militarily, politically, and in every other way, Saladin was the most successful leader of the period. His successes were so surprising and total that historians sometimes invoke luck and good fortune to explain them. However, as I have studied Saladin, I am convinced he succeeded in war for a much deeper reason—a reason that won't seem at first to be related to war at all."

"What?" Pettis asked. "What reason?"

"To understand it," Yusuf said, "we need to get a better feel for the man. Let me tell you a story. On one occasion, an army scout came to Saladin with a distressed woman from the enemy camp. She had requested, hysterically, that the scout take her to Saladin. She threw herself before Saladin and said, 'Yesterday some Muslim thieves entered my tent and stole my little girl. I cried all through the night, believing I would never see her again. But our commanders told me that you, the king of the Muslims, are merciful.' She begged for his help."

Lou considered getting up for another coffee but decided to remain seated.

"Saladin was moved to tears," Yusuf continued. "He immediately sent one of his men to the slave market to look for the girl. They located her within the hour and returned her to her mother, whom they then escorted back to the enemy camp."

Yusuf paused for a moment. "If you were to research Saladin, you would discover that this story is characteristic. He was renowned for his kindness toward allies and enemies alike."

"I'm not sure those who died at the end of his army's swords thought him kind," Elizabeth said. "But I agree that in comparison to others of the period, he did shine a little brighter."

Lou was unimpressed. His mind drifted back to Vietnam and to all the dead young men his regiment had to carry out of the jungles. When he had returned from Vietnam, Lou made a personal point of visiting the mother of each soldier who had lost his life under his command. Over a period of two years, he visited fifty-three towns, from Seattle, Washington, and San Diego, California, in the West; to Portland, Maine, in the East; and Savannah, Georgia, in the South. He sat in the living rooms of the homes these men never returned to and held their grieving mothers in his arms as he told them of the heroic deeds of their sons. He loved his men. He never stopped dreaming of ways he could have saved more of them. *Being kind and merciful sounds nice,* he thought, *but they are traits that are poorly rewarded in wartime.*

"With that bit of background," Yusuf continued, "let me contrast Saladin's recapture of Jerusalem with the Crusaders' initial invasion. In the spring of 1187, after the Crusaders had broken a truce, Saladin called upon the forces of Islam to gather in Damascus. He planned to march against the occupiers in a unified effort and drive them from their lands."

"If I might," Elizabeth said, "who was occupying whom was not entirely clear. As I mentioned before, each side viewed the other as an occupying force."

"Right," Yusuf said. "Sorry for the imprecision. Saladin sprung a trap on the occupying—err, rather, Western—forces near the Sea of Galilee. A few escaped, including a leader named Balian of Ibelin. Balian escaped to Tyre, where via messenger he made a surprising request of Saladin: he asked whether he could go to Jerusalem and fetch his wife and bring her back to safety in Tyre. He promised he would not take up arms in defense of Jerusalem. Saladin agreed."

Lou fought the urge to steer the conversation toward Vietnam.

"However," Yusuf continued, "upon arriving in Jerusalem and finding there was no one to lead its defense, Balian begged Saladin to let him out of his commitment. He wanted to stay and lead the resistance against Saladin's army. Saladin not only allowed it, he sent an escort to lead Balian's wife from Jerusalem to the safety of Tyre!"

Lou let out an audible groan.

"Yes, Lou, kind of hard to imagine, isn't it?"

"She must have been a looker, that's all I can say." Lou glanced around for a laugh. Miguel obliged him, but for the rest the joke fell flat. Carol shook her head ever so slightly and fought to remember that Lou was better on the inside than his outward bravado sometimes suggested. She knew that his behavior was being exacerbated by the stress he was feeling from having to be away from work when so much was going wrong there.

"The siege of Jerusalem began on the twentieth of September," Yusuf said. "Nine days later, Saladin's men breached the wall close to the place where the Crusaders had flowed through almost ninety years earlier. Saladin put his men under strict order not to harm a single Christian person or plunder any of their possessions. He reinforced the guards at Christian places of worship and announced that the defeated peoples would be welcome to come to Jerusalem on pilgrimage whenever they liked."

Yusuf paused and Lou took the opportunity to refill his coffee. He could tell he was going to need it.

"As a way to restock the treasury and in keeping with war practices of the time, Saladin worked out a ransom structure with Balian for each of the city's inhabitants. His men protested that the amounts were absurdly low. But Saladin was concerned for the poor among them. So much so, in fact, that he let many leave without any ransom whatsoever. He sent widows and children away with gifts. His leaders objected, saying that if they were going to let so many leave without any compensation, they should at least increase the ransom for the wealthy. But Saladin refused. Balian himself was allowed to leave with most of his wealth. Saladin even sent an escort to protect him on his journey to Tyre."

Yusuf looked around at the group.

"He sounds disturbingly weak to me," Lou said.

"Yes," Yusuf said, "so weak that he was the most successful military leader of his era and remains revered to this day."

"He's still weak. And I doubt his capabilities as a leader."

"Why do you say that, Lou?" Elizabeth said.

"Well," Lou began, "you heard what Yusuf said. He let all those people take advantage of him."

"You mean because he spared their lives?" Elizabeth asked.

"And let them make off with the treasury."

"But they weren't in it for the treasury," she said. "They were trying to establish a lasting victory."

"Then why not get rid of their enemies?" Lou said. "Let them walk away and you just allow them to fight another day. Trust me, I fought in Vietnam. We would have been massacred there if we took the soft approach."

Pettis spoke up. "We were massacred in Vietnam, Lou."

Lou's back went rigid. With eyes smoldering, he turned hard on Pettis. "Listen, Pettis, why don't you stick to what you know? You have no idea what Vietnam was about—or about the heroism our men showed there."

"Air force—eighth Tactical Fighter Wing. Two tours." Pettis looked calmly at Lou. "You?"

Lou was surprised, but he felt little connection to Pettis, despite sharing a war. "Four years. Second Battalion, Ninth Marines," Lou said. "Hell in a Helmet, as we called ourselves. Sorry."

"No apology necessary," Pettis said.

"Two veterans in the group," Yusuf said enthusiastically. "Splendid!

"Lou," he continued, "you mentioned that Saladin sounds weak or soft."

Lou nodded.

"Do you suppose, however, that the defenders of the cities he captured one by one thought him weak? That the rival Muslim leaders he subdued thought him weak? That those who had been defeated by no one else thought him weak?"

Lou hesitated. "I suppose not, but it's all about context."

"No, they surely wouldn't have," Yusuf said. "And the reason why is simple: he wasn't weak. He was, in fact, remarkably and unfailingly strong. But he was something more than—or perhaps more accurately, deeper than—strong. And this extra something is what set him apart from all the others of his era who, although strong, were unsuccessful."

Yusuf paused.

"What was it?" Pettis asked. "This something extra, this something deeper."

"The most important factor in helping things go right," Yusuf said.

"Which is?" Pettis said.

"The secret of Saladin's success in war," Yusuf continued, "was that his heart was at peace."

This was too much for Lou. "'Heart at peace' you say, Yusuf?" The edge to his voice was back. "That's your secret—that Saladin's heart was at peace?"

"Yes."

"You've got to be kidding," he said, looking first at Pettis and then at the others, searching for allies. He thought he found what he was looking for in Pettis, who seemed lost in thought, his brow deeply furrowed.

Lou then glanced at Elizabeth but couldn't read her expression. He dug in once more, keeping her in his sight as he spoke. "So the secret to war is to have a heart at peace?"

"Yes, Lou." Yusuf looked serious. "And not just in war. It is the secret to success in business and family life as well. The state of your heart toward your children—whether at peace or at war—is by far the most important factor in this intervention we are now undertaking. It is also what will most determine your ability to successfully maneuver your company through the challenges created by your recent defections."

This comment knocked Lou completely off his stride. He was not accustomed to people standing up to his sarcasm, and Yusuf's even bolder development of his thesis and his pointed comment about Lou's corporate troubles caught Lou off guard.

He looked sideways at Carol, whom he surmised to have been the source of the inside information. She stared stiffly ahead, not acknowledging his gaze.

# 4 • BENEATH BEHAVIOR

Just then, one of the young employees of the company walked into the room and whispered something to Yusuf. Excusing himself, Yusuf quickly followed the staff member out of the room.

After he left, Pettis said to Avi, "I'm not sure what Yusuf meant by a heart being at peace. I'd like to hear more about that."

"Sure," Avi said. "To begin with, let's compare Saladin's recapture of Jerusalem to the earlier capture by the Crusaders." He looked at Pettis. "Do you notice any differences in the two victories?"

"Certainly," Pettis said. "The Crusaders acted like barbarians."

"And Saladin?"

"He was almost humane," Pettis said. "For someone who was attacking, anyway."

"Say more about what you mean by *humane.*"

Pettis paused to gather his thoughts. "What I mean, I think, is that Saladin seems to have had regard for the people he was defeating. Whereas the crusading forces seem—well, they seem to have been barbaric, as I said before. They just massacred all those people, without regard for human life."

"Exactly," Avi agreed. "To the initial crusading forces, the people *didn't* matter. That is, the Crusaders didn't really regard them as people so much as objects or chattel to be driven or exterminated at will. Saladin, on the other hand, saw and honored the humanity of those he conquered. He may have wished they had never come to Jerusalem, but he recognized these were people he was doing battle with and that he therefore had to see, treat, and honor them as such."

"So what does that have to do with us?" Lou asked. "You're talking about a 900-year-old story, and a story about war at that. What does it have to do with our kids?" Thinking of what Yusuf had said about his company, he added, "Or our employees?"

Avi looked squarely at Lou. "In every moment, we are choosing to be either like Saladin or like the crusading invaders. In the way we regard our children, our spouses, neighbors, colleagues, and strangers, we choose to see others either as people like ourselves or as objects. They either count like we do or they don't. In the former case, since we regard them as we regard ourselves, we say our hearts are at peace toward them. In the latter case, since we see them as objects, we say our hearts are at war."

"You seem to be pretty taken by Muslims' humanity toward others and others' inhumanity toward Muslims," Lou said. "I'm afraid that's naïve." He thought of what he knew of Avi's history. "And surprising, coming from someone whose own father was killed by the people you are praising."

Avi heaved a heavy sigh. "Yusuf and I have been speaking of no one, Lou, but Saladin. There are those who see humanely and those who don't in every country and faith community. Lumping every-one of a particular race or culture or faith into a single stereotype is a way of failing to see them as people. We are trying, here, to avoid that mistake, and it seems that Saladin is a person we could learn from."

Lou fell silent in the face of this rebuke. He was beginning to feel lonely among the group. He wondered if Pettis was buying all this peace and love talk.

"The contrast between Saladin's taking of Jerusalem and the Crusaders' taking of Jerusalem," Avi continued, "teaches an important lesson: almost any behavior—even behavior as stark as war—can be done in two different ways." At this, he went to the board and drew the following:

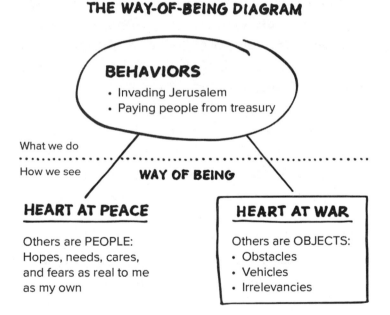

## THE WAY-OF-BEING DIAGRAM

**BEHAVIORS**
- Invading Jerusalem
- Paying people from treasury

What we do

How we see    **WAY OF BEING**

**HEART AT PEACE**

Others are PEOPLE:
Hopes, needs, cares,
and fears as real to me
as my own

**HEART AT WAR**

Others are OBJECTS:
- Obstacles
- Vehicles
- Irrelevancies

"Think about it," Avi said, turning to face the group. "The Saladin story suggests that there is something deeper than our behavior—something we call our *way of being*. Martin Buber was a Jewish philosopher who was born in Austria but lived much of his life in Jerusalem. He explored extensively how our way of being is inextricably tied to the way we see and regard other people. He demonstrated that at all times, no matter what we might be doing, we are either 'I-It' or 'I-Thou.' In other words, who we are is determined by how we see others. We are always seeing others either as objects—as obstacles, for example, or as vehicles or irrelevancies—or we are seeing them as people. And how we see others determines our own way of being. To put it in terms of the Saladin story, there are two ways to take Jerusalem: from people or from objects."

"Who cares how you take it, then?" Lou blurted, suddenly feeling energized for another round. "If you have to take it, you have to take it. It's just that simple. A soldier doesn't have the luxury of worrying about the life of the person who is staring down his lance or barrel. In fact, it would be dangerous to invite him to consider that life. He might hesitate when he needs to fire."

This comment crystallized a doubt that had been creeping up within Pettis as well. "Lou's right," he said. "What about that?" he asked Avi. "Lou's worry about soldiers seeing their enemies as people is legitimate, is it not? I see problems with that as well."

"It seems like it might be a problem, doesn't it? But was it a problem for Saladin?"

"Yes, it was," Lou said, emboldened by Pettis's support. "He compromised his people by allowing the enemy to leave with Jerusalem's riches. That's not leadership—it's weakness."

"Do you suppose seeing others as people means that we have to let them leave with riches? That it means we must let others take advantage of us?"

"Well, it seems like it does, yes," Lou said. "At least, that's what it seems you've been implying."

"No, that's not his point," Elizabeth said, staring at the diagram. "You have the behaviors at the top and the two basic ways of seeing others at the bottom. Avi's saying that everything he's written in the behavior area—taking Jerusalem, for example, or paying people from the treasury—can be done in either of those ways of being, with a heart at peace or a heart at war."

"Well then who cares which way you do it?" Lou repeated. "If you need to take Jerusalem, just take Jerusalem. Who cares which way you do it? Just get the job done!"

Avi looked thoughtfully at Lou. "Cory cares," he said.

"Huh?"

"Cory cares."

"He cares about *what?*"

"He cares whether he's being seen as a person or an object."

Lou didn't say anything.

"Seeing an equal person as an inferior object is an act of violence, Lou. It hurts as much as a punch to the face. In fact, in many ways it hurts more. Bruises heal more quickly than emotional scars do."

"I never lost any soldiers to bruised egos," Lou said. He wanted to say more, but he slouched back in his chair and thought about Cory.

"The inhabitants of Jerusalem surely cared how they were seen and treated. But even more than that, you care, Lou. You care whether you are being seen as a person or as an object. In fact, there is little you care more about than this."

"Then you don't know anything about me." Lou shook his head in disagreement. "I couldn't care less what others think about me. Just ask my wife."

The sad irony of his comment, as autobiographical as it was on this particular day, didn't penetrate Lou. At his side, Carol blushed slightly, clearly unsettled by the attention she felt was suddenly directed at her.

Avi smiled good-naturedly. "Actually, Lou, I think you do care."

"Then you think wrong."

"Maybe," Avi continued. "It wouldn't be the first time. But here's something to consider: has it been important to you to get others to agree with you this morning?"

Lou remembered his earlier hope that Elizabeth shared his views and the energy he felt when it appeared that Pettis did.

"If so, you do care. But ultimately, you are the only one who will be able to answer that question."

Lou felt a tinge of pain, the way one does when a foot or limb has been asleep and is just beginning to revive itself.

"This way of being is of great practical importance. First of all, think of a difficult business situation—say a complicated negotiation, for example. Who do you think would be more likely to put together a deal in difficult circumstances: a negotiator who sees the others in the negotiation as objects or one who sees them as people?"

This question piqued Lou's interest, as he was in the middle of a union negotiation that was going nowhere.

"The one who sees others as people," Carl said. "Definitely."

"Why?" Avi asked.

"Because," Teri said, "whether you're talking about negotiators or anyone else, people don't like dealing with jerks. It's human nature to gravitate toward nice people and to poke mean people in the eye." She glanced toward Lou.

Avi chuckled. "That's true, isn't it? In fact, have you noticed that we sometimes choose to poke another in the eye even when doing so harms our own position?"

This question swept Lou's thoughts back to an emergency meeting just two weeks earlier. Kate Stenarude, Jack Taylor, Nelson Mumford, Kirk Weir, and Don Shilling—five of Lou's six key executives—were standing in their places at Zagrum Company's boardroom table, giving Lou an earful. They would leave, they told him, unless Lou gave them more space to run their departments. They called him a meddler, a micromanager, and a control freak. One of them (Jack Taylor, Lou vowed never to forget) even painted Lou a tyrant.

Lou had listened to all of them in silence, not even looking into their faces. But he was burning inside. Ingrates! he had growled to himself. *Incompetent, bumbling, turncoat ingrates!*

"Get the hell out then!" he had finally yelled. "If the standards here are too high for you, then you'd better leave now because they're not coming down!"

"We're not talking about the standards, Lou," Kate had pleaded. "We're talking about the atmosphere of oppression we've come to work under. The ladder thing you just pulled on me, for example." She was referring to how Lou had recently removed a ladder from the sales team area, an act that symbolically undercut her attempt to implement a new incentive system in her department. "It's a small thing, but it speaks volumes."

"It's only oppressive for those who can't measure up to the standards, Kate."

"Again," said Kate, "this isn't about the standards—"

Lou cut her off. "And honestly, Kate, after all I've done for you." He shook his head in disgust. "You wouldn't have made it this far without me. Show a little respect. I would have expected more out of you."

Nobody came to his aid so he doubled down: "So get out then! All of you. Get the hell out!"

The March Meltdown, as this interchange and subsequent defection had come to be called around the halls of Zagrum Company, had nearly ground Zagrum's work to a halt over the last two weeks. Lou was worried about his company's future.

"Viewed economically," Avi continued, "this is an insane strategy. But we do it anyway. In fact, it's almost like we feel compelled to do it. We can get ourselves in a position where we compulsively act in ways that make our own lives more difficult—by stoking the fires of resentment in a spouse, for example, or fostering anger in a child. But we do it anyway. Which leads us to the first reason why way of being is so important: when our hearts are at war, we can't see clearly. We give ourselves the best opportunity to make clear-minded decisions only to the extent that our hearts are at peace."

Lou thought about that as he pondered his decisions regarding Kate and the others who had left the company.

"Here's another reason why way of being is so important," Avi said. "Think about the negotiation situation again. The most successful negotiators understand the other side's concerns and worries as much as their own. But who is more likely to be able to consider and understand the other side's positions so fully: the person who sees others as objects or the person who sees them as people?"

"The one who sees people," Ria answered. Pettis and most of the others nodded in agreement.

"I think that's right," Avi said. "People whose hearts are at war toward others can't consider others' objections and challenges enough to be able to find a way through them."

Lou thought of the impasse with the union.

"Finally," Avi said, "let me add a third reason why way of being is important. Think about your experiences over the last few years with the children you have brought to us. Have you ever felt like they reacted unfairly to you even when you were bending over backwards to be kind and fair to them?"

Lou's mind drifted back to an exchange he and Cory had just two mornings earlier. "So it's all my fault, right, Dad? You're the great Lou Herbert who has never made a mistake in his life, right?"

"Don't be a child," Lou remembered responding, proud that he was able to remain so calm in the face of such disrespect.

"It must be pretty embarrassing having a son like me—an addict, a thief. Right?"

Lou didn't say anything, and he congratulated himself for rising above the moment. As he thought about it, however, he had to admit Cory was right. Lou was distinctly proud of his two older children—Mary, twenty-four, a PhD candidate at MIT; and Jesse, twenty-two, a senior at Lou's alma mater, Syracuse University. In comparison, he found Cory embarrassing. That was true.

"Well, let me tell you something, *Officer Daaaad*. Being the son of Lou Herbert is a living hell, to tell you the truth. Do you know what it feels like knowing that your dad thinks you're a loser? I was never as good as Mary or Jesse. At least, not to you. Well, let me tell you something. You're not as good as Mom, or any other adult I know, for that matter. You're a bigger loser as a parent than I'll ever be as a son. And you're just as much of a disaster at work. Why else would Kate and the others have walked out on you?"

This exchange had once again showed Lou that treating Cory civilly got him nowhere. Cory disrespected him whether Lou yelled or stayed silent.

"I'm going to suggest something to you about this," Avi continued. "It's an idea you might want to resist at first, especially regarding your children. But here it is: generally speaking, we respond to others' way of being toward us rather than to their behavior. Which is to say that our children respond more to how we're regarding them than they do to our particular words or actions. We can treat our children fairly, for example, but if our hearts are warring toward them while we're doing it, they won't think they're being treated fairly at all. In fact, they'll respond to us as if they were being attacked."

Avi looked at the group. "As important as behavior is, most problems at home, at work, and in the world are not failures of strategy but failures of being. As we've discussed, when our hearts are at war, we can't see situations clearly, we can't consider others' positions seriously enough to solve difficult problems, and we end up provoking hurtful behavior in others."

Lou was not buying this. His mouth was dry again and he needed more coffee.

"If we have deep problems," Avi continued, "it's because we are failing at the deepest part of the solution. And when we fail at this deepest level, we invite our own failure."

# 5 • THE PATTERN OF CONFLICT

"Actually," Avi said, "when our hearts are at war, we not only invite failure, we *invest* in it. Let me give you an example. One Saturday, I returned home at about 5:45 p.m., just fifteen minutes before I was to meet a friend for tennis. Problem was, I had also promised my wife, Hannah, that I would mow the lawn."

There were a few knowing chuckles around the room.

"Well, I raced to the garage, pulled out the lawn mower, and mowed it in a sprint. I then ran back into the house to get dressed for tennis. As I raced past Hannah toward the stairs, I mumbled that I was going to meet my friend Paul for a game of tennis. I was just about to the stairs when Hannah called after me, 'Are you going to edge?'"

Lou looked at Carol, wondering if the story was reaching her.

Avi continued: "I stopped in my tracks. 'It doesn't need edging,' I said. 'Not this time.'

"'I think it does,' she said."

Carol nodded.

"'Oh, come on,' I said. 'No one is going to pass our house and say, "Look, Marge, the Rozens didn't edge!"' This didn't sway her in the least, so I added, 'Besides, I ran the wheels of the mower up on the cement as I cut around the edges. It looks fine.'

"'You said you were going to mow,' she said, 'and that means edging too.'"

Carol looked restless. She stood up and walked toward the refreshments table.

"'No, it doesn't!' I told my wife. 'Mowing means mowing; edging means edging. You don't have to edge every time you mow. That's ridiculous. Besides, I'm already late for tennis. Paul is waiting. Is that what you want?'

"I thought I had her at that," Avi continued, "but then she said, 'Okay, I guess *I'll* edge then.'"

The knowing chuckles returned. "Guilt-tripping you, wasn't she?" Miguel spoke up for the first time that morning, in a husky voice that matched his appearance. His wife, Ria, didn't look too pleased by the comment.

"Exactly," Avi said. "I didn't want her doing it, so I told her that maybe I could edge when I got back. And with that, I threw on my tennis gear and left. I didn't get home until after dark. I'd beaten Paul for the first time and was feeling pretty happy. I went into the kitchen, opened the fridge, and poured myself a large glass of orange juice. Hannah walked into the room when I was in the middle of a long guzzle. I quickly dropped the glass from my mouth and was about to say, 'I beat Paul!' when she asked, 'Are you going to edge?'"

Carol sat back down and locked eyes with Lou. She wondered what he was making of this story.

"The excitement drained from me in an instant," Avi said. "I was immediately back in the irritated emotional place I had been a couple of hours earlier. 'You've been sitting around here wondering for the last two hours whether I'm going to edge?' I said. 'That's pathetic.'

"'But you said you would when you got back,' she replied."

"Better do what she says," Miguel said.

Avi smiled. "I shot back at her: 'I said *maybe* I would. But that was before I knew it was going to be pitch black.'"

"But you said you'd do it," Ria said. "You made an agreement."

"That's exactly what she said," Avi continued. "So I said, 'Do you want me to put out my eye or something? It's dark out. I can't wear my sunglasses.'

"'Then *I'll* edge,' she said."

"Hell, let her do it!" Lou bellowed. "If she wants it done that badly, she should just do it herself."

A few people chuckled at that, Miguel especially. Carol pursed her lips.

"Well, I didn't do that, Lou," Avi said. "Instead, I raised my head piously high, inhaled deeply, and said, 'Okay. I'll edge to keep peace in the family.' And then I stalked to the garage, pulled out the weed eater, and edged for two solid hours. If she wanted edging, she was going to get edging!"

A few in the group laughed at that as well.

"But think about it," Avi continued. "When I came back in the house, do you think my edging had kept peace in the family?"

The participants all shook their heads—even Lou, although he was barely aware of it.

"And it didn't keep peace in the family for one simple reason: my heart was still at war toward Hannah. She seemed just as small-minded, inconsiderate, demanding, unreasonable, and cold when I was edging as when I wasn't. The change in my outward behavior didn't change how I was feeling about her. In fact, if anything, the more I edged in the darkness, the worse she seemed to me. When I chewed up a piece of the fence because I couldn't see well, I felt a perverse sense of satisfaction. It proved how unreasonable Hannah was being."

Lou and Pettis began nodding.

"As you might imagine, when I finally came back in the house, our feelings toward each other poked through every word, look, and gesture. In fact, if anything, we were less civil to each other than before—which ticked me off all the more, by the way. Here I had put my own eyesight, or at least my property, at risk by doing what she unreasonably demanded, and she was still mad at me! *The least she could do is be grateful,* I told myself. *But no, she's impossible to please!*"

Miguel started coughing in laughter. He brought his barrel-shaped fist to his mouth to try to quell the eruption.

"What is it, Miguel?" Avi asked.

He raised his hand in front of him, telling Avi to wait a moment while he got himself under control.

Avi broke out into a big grin himself as he watched Miguel struggle to gather himself.

Clearing his throat, Miguel finally said in a pinched voice, "Sorry. Your story reminded me of something," he said. "Happened two nights ago."

Ria's eyes widened as she turned to look at him.

"I had to do the dishes. Knew Ria would be really upset if I didn't. Even though I had to work early in the morning. And then, when I finished, she came in. Started snooping. Wanted to see if I'd done it...correctly."

"I did not!" Ria said.

"Yes, you did," Miguel said. "Like always."

"I was just coming in to get something to eat."

"Right," he chuckled. "That's why you were looking in the sink? For food?"

The group looked toward Ria, half of them siding with her in this retelling of their domestic dispute.

Ria's face started to turn pink. "Well, I wouldn't have to do that if you would just clean up like you should."

Miguel shook his head.

"I take it you mentioned this, Miguel," Avi interrupted, "because you felt these warring feelings we're talking about?"

"That's right. But who wouldn't feel angry? Right? She just said it herself." He pointed at Ria. "She's always hovering. Checks what I do. Doesn't think it's good enough."

Carol stirred beside Lou and said, "Maybe she's not hovering, Miguel. Maybe she's just tired of having to do everything."

Lou was aghast, partly because he was feeling a kinship with Miguel at the moment and partly because it was so unlike Carol to put someone on the spot. He spoke up. "Really, Carol? Maybe this woman should be grateful her man does the dishes even though he carries the burden of making a living."

"Oh, so women don't have their share of burdens, Lou?" It was Gwyn. She had seemed to Lou so restrained this morning, but she had tired of Lou's domination of the dialogue and could restrain herself no longer. "We work—we just don't get equal pay," she continued. "And who said that Miguel is the breadwinner? Are you living so far in the past that you believe women don't make money? Perhaps women don't even have names in your mind. Maybe we're all just *this woman* or *that woman*. Maybe I'm just that *Black* woman. Is that the way it is? Should we all just be happy for what we're able to do for you? Is that how it is in your house? Is that how it is at your company? Is there even a woman on your executive team? Surely not a Black one." Gwyn knew that this interjection would play right into the "angry Black woman" trope, but she didn't care. Someone had to say something.

Lou felt blindsided and was about to retort that he in fact did have a woman on the team when he remembered again that Kate was gone. "Hearts at war," Avi broke in. "That's what we're talking about. Lou, Gwyn, Carol, Miguel, Ria, the rest of us—do you feel what I mean? How are we seeing each other—right now? As allies? As enemies? These are warring feelings."

Avi paused for a moment. "Go ahead, look around," he said. "Are we seeing people, or are we seeing objects?"

Most in the room avoided each other's eyes despite the invitation to look. Lou fought the urge to defend himself and looked at his shoes instead.

"When we start seeing others as objects, we begin provoking them to make our lives difficult. We actually start inviting others to make us miserable. We begin provoking in others the very things we say we hate."

"How so?" Lou asked.

"Can't you feel it?" Avi said. "How our emotions are beginning to run away from us and how we are beginning to provoke hostile feelings and comments in each other?"

Lou had to admit he could feel it, but he said nothing.

"We see the same pattern in my story with Hannah," Avi continued. "Let's diagram it, and I think you'll see what I mean. To begin with, Hannah asked me to edge, didn't she? And then complained and badgered me when I objected." He then drew the following on the board:

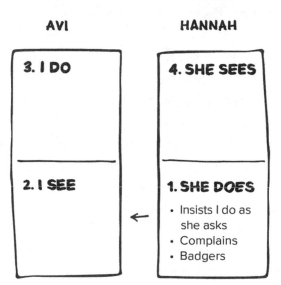

## THE COLLUSION DIAGRAM

"Why are you calling this collusion?" Pettis asked.

"For reasons that will become clearer in a few minutes. Make sure I come back to that, will you?"

Pettis nodded.

"When Hannah asked me to edge, how do you suppose I began to see or regard her?"

"As demanding," Miguel said. Glancing at Ria, he added, "Unreasonable too."

Avi wrote this in the area he had marked with a 2.

"Let's face it," Lou said, "she was a nag, plain and simple. Not saying she always is; Hannah's probably a wonderful lady. But in this case, she should have just done it herself or stopped complaining."

"Okay, Lou." Avi chuckled as he added "nag" to the board. "You're very direct. Now, would it be fair to say I was seeing her as an object?"

"As an obstacle, definitely," Lou said.

Avi added this as well.

"So when I was seeing Hannah in the ways we've listed here at number 2—as a nag and so on—how did I act? What did I do?"

"You protested," Gwyn said. "You didn't think you should have to do it, and you told her so. A bit childishly too I might add."

Avi smiled. "Yes, that's exactly what I did."

"So I protested," Avi repeated, adding this in the area he had marked as number 3. "What else did I do?"

"I would say you were trying to help her see the situation more reasonably," Teri said. "I don't think you were being childish necessarily. Bothered, certainly, but not childish. After all, you mowed even though you didn't have the time. You were just trying to make your appointment."

"Yes, *his* appointment," Gwyn said. "That's just the point. He wanted to play tennis with a friend, but maybe she had plans of her own. What about what she wanted to do? Shouldn't that matter?"

"Okay, Gwyn, tell me," Lou interjected. "What plans of Hannah's required that Avi edge the lawn, and right then? What would that have to do with *her* plans, assuming she had any?"

"'Assuming she had any?'" Gwyn gave a sharp laugh. "Can't women have plans, Lou?"

"Of course they can have plans. That's not what I'm saying. But don't make plans that require my involvement. Don't try to run my life and then act like I'm violating your rights if I don't do just what you want me to do."

Carol closed her eyes, hoping she could will her husband to shut up. She was willing to put up with his chauvinism at home, but this public display was embarrassing.

"Gwyn, Lou," Avi said in an imploring tone, "let's hold on here. We might disagree about a lot of things, but how we do it makes a big difference. If we start seeing each other as objects, we'll get to the point where we'll need to see each other as disagreeable rather than as simply disagreeing. Once that happens, we'll end up provoking each other just as Hannah and I did. Let's not fall into the very trap we're seeking to understand and avoid."

This comment, like Avi's invitation a couple of minutes earlier, appeared to lessen some of the rancor in the room. But Avi knew this was mostly illusion. Anger—or more precisely, war—was brewing just beneath the surface and threatening to sweep away their thoughts and emotions.

"Let's come back to the story," he said. "So I protested to Hannah," he continued, pointing at the area marked 3, "and tried to teach her. And then, of course, I even ended up edging. In fact, I edged with a kind of ferocious intensity, didn't I—with an attitude?"

Most in the room nodded and Avi added "Teach her," and "Comply with attitude," to number 3 on the diagram.

"Given how I acted and how I was seeing Hannah, how do you suppose she saw me?"

"As self-centered," Gwyn answered.

"And inconsiderate," said Ria.

"And immature," added Gwyn.

"Yes, okay. Thanks. I think," Avi smiled, adding these comments to area 4. "So let's look at this situation," he said, backing away from the board.

## THE COLLUSION DIAGRAM

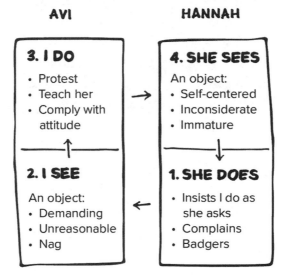

**AVI**                                  **HANNAH**

**3. I DO**

- Protest
- Teach her
- Comply with attitude

**4. SHE SEES**

An object:
- Self-centered
- Inconsiderate
- Immature

**2. I SEE**

An object:
- Demanding
- Unreasonable
- Nag

**1. SHE DOES**

- Insists I do as she asks
- Complains
- Badgers

"If Hannah is seeing me as we've listed here at number 4—as self-centered, inconsiderate, and immature—is she now less or more likely to insist that I do as she says and to complain when I don't?"

"More," the group answered.

"So she'll do more of what we've listed here at number 1, which means that I'll see and do more of what we've listed at numbers

2 and 3, and she'll then see and do more of what we've listed at numbers 4 and 1! Around and around we'll go, each of us provoking in the other the very things we're complaining about." He paused to let that settle. "Think about it. Each of us ends up inviting the very behaviors we say we hate in the other!"

"But that's crazy," Pettis said. "And familiar."

"Yes, Pettis, it is crazy. And because it is, we call this *collusion* rather than merely *conflict.*"

Pettis puzzled on that. "I'm not sure I understand the distinction."

"The word 'conflict' is passive," Avi said. "It is something that happens *to* us. For example, something we refer to as a conflict might simply be the result of a misunderstanding. But many conflicts aren't that way at all. Many conflicts are like the one we've been considering: they involve situations where the parties are actively engaged in perpetuating the trouble. In such cases, far from being passive victims of misunderstanding, we become active perpetuators of misunderstanding. The word 'collusion' captures this element of active participation more accurately than 'conflict' does, so we use it to describe conflicts where the parties are actually inviting the very things they're fighting against." At this, Avi wrote the following on the board:

## COLLUSION

A conflict where the parties are inviting the very things they're fighting against

"And you're right—this is insane." Avi put the cap on his marker and scanned over the group. "And yet this insanity prevails in large areas of our lives. It describes much of what happens between spouses who are struggling, parents and children who are battling, coworkers who are competing, and countries that are fighting." Avi stopped talking and took a deep breath. "It also describes what has been happening in this room, doesn't it? We're beginning to provoke in others the very comments and behaviors we are accusing them of. Granted, loading your children into a van this morning probably put a lot of you on edge."

The entire group seemed to agree with this last point.

"Despite the insanity of it," Avi continued, "this pattern of interpersonal and inner violence can come to rule our lives and influence the organizations and countries where we work and live. In fact, this insanity tries to spread. Let me show you how."

# 6 · ESCALATION

"Look around the room," Avi invited once more. "Who would you want to gather with and talk to if we were to take a break? Go ahead," he invited. "Look around."

Gwyn glanced furtively at Ria and Carol. Miguel looked quickly at Lou but then turned away when Lou turned toward him. Lou looked inquiringly at Elizabeth, but she didn't acknowledge him. She seemed not to want to be included.

"And what would you be likely to talk about with these people?"

There was silence in the room, but eyes darted here and there, and it was clear to Avi that the group was responding silently to his question.

"Gwyn," Avi said, interrupting the silence, "if I might be so bold as to ask, who in the room would you most like to talk to, and what do you think your conversations might be about?"

"Oh, probably Ria, I'd say. And maybe Carol. And we'd talk about their husbands, I'd imagine." She smiled. "And definitely mine."

"And what about their husbands?" Avi asked.

"I think we'd compare horror stories."

Avi butted in before Lou could fire back.

"Notice what's happened here. Gwyn ends up talking with Ria and Carol. And about what? About how they are each being treated unfairly or unjustly by someone else. We end up gathering with allies—actual, perceived, or potential—as a way of feeling justified in our own accusing views of others."

A few heads nodded.

"As a result of this fact," Avi continued, "conflicts spread and escalate."

Adding more boxes to the diagram on the board, he said, "Like this."

## THE COLLUSION DIAGRAM

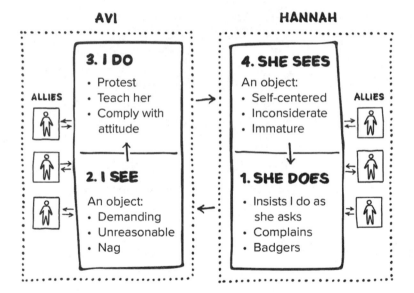

"So what begins as a conflict between two people spreads to a conflict between many as each person enlists others to their side. Everyone begins acting in ways that invite more of the very problem from the other side that each is complaining about! We have seen it happen here in this room in the last few minutes. It certainly happened that way in my home as Hannah and I found ways to recruit our children into the fray. I would conspicuously roll my eyes, for example, when Hannah demanded something of me. And I would commiserate with the children when I thought she was coming down too hard on them. I recruited my kids into feeling mistreated like I felt."

"That is twisted," Ria said.

"Yes, it is." Avi put the marker down. "And I'd bet that if you work in an organization, it looks like this as well—with employees recruiting colleagues and others with the tales they tell, leading to an organization that is divided into warring silos, one group complaining incessantly about another, and the other returning the same. Until finally, your organization is filled with people whose energies are largely spent on sustaining conflict—what we call collusion—and who therefore are not fully focused on achieving the productive goals of the organization."

The group remained silent.

"Am I right?" Avi asked.

Although he didn't say anything, Lou had to admit that he saw this same pattern in spades at Zagrum. He could also see himself and Cory spinning in the same kind of cycle. The harder he was on Cory, the more Cory rebelled, and the more Cory rebelled, the more Lou bore down on him. Lou didn't roll his eyes like Avi did, but he gathered allies by complaining about Cory to any member of the family willing to listen.

"It seems to me like many global conflicts are collusions as well," Elizabeth said. "The conflict in my region of the world, in Northern Ireland, for example. Both sides are inviting the very things they're fighting against. It doesn't end."

Avi nodded. "It's the same way in the conflict between Israelis and Palestinians. In fact, the concept of collusion explains how an ancient personal conflict now threatens the entire world. Consider the story of Abraham and his sons Isaac and Ishmael. These sons, in accordance with decrees attributed in scripture to God, became fathers of nations—Isaac, the father of the Israelite people, and Ishmael, the father of the Arab people. As such, these men hold special places in the belief systems of Jews, Christians, and Muslims the world over."

Avi paused. Nobody jumped in so he continued. "Jews and Christians, for their part, believe that Isaac was the chosen son with specific rights granted to him and his posterity, including rights to the land. They believe that God told Abraham to offer Isaac as a sacrifice as a test of Abraham's faith. According to the Old Testament, this sacrifice was to take place on a hill 'in the land of Moriah'—a location in present-day Jerusalem. Centuries later, King Solomon constructed a temple on a hill in Jerusalem believed to be the location of this event, a mount known as Mount Moriah— the mountain after which Camp Moriah is named. In modern times, this mount is capped by the Al Aqsa Mosque complex, originally constructed by the Muslims after the initial conquest of Jerusalem that we talked about earlier. The world-famous shrine known as the Dome of the Rock, located within the thirty-five-acre complex, occupies the spot from where Muslims believe the prophet Mohammed ascended to heaven in a nocturnal vision. It is also believed to be the place of the experience between Abraham and his son. Which brings us to Ishmael."

"Are we going to relate this to *our* lives?" Lou asked.

"Yes," Carl said. "How do we stop…collusion, as you call it, in our homes?"

"I'm getting there," Avi said. "In this example, although the Koran does not tell us one way or the other, many Muslims believe it was Ishmael, not Isaac, that Abraham was commanded to sacrifice on Moriah. Muslims also believe that Ishmael, rather than Isaac, was the chosen son. And finally, they believe it was Ishmael, not Isaac, who was given the right to the land. And so we have a dispute between brothers—those who believe Isaac was the chosen son and those who believe Ishmael is the chosen one. Descendants of each believe that they have claim to the land and to the heritage and primary blessings of the prophet Abraham."

Avi pointed at the Collusion Diagram. "How does this relate to us? Well, you could substitute Isaac for my name and Ishmael for Hannah's and the diagram would be equally true of that conflict. Believers on each side now provoke the very mistreatment from the other that they are complaining about."

"But what if one of the views is the correct one, Avi?" Lou said. "Are you suggesting that all parties in a conflict are equally in the wrong, even if one side's claims are patently false?"

"And which side's claims are patently false here, Lou?" The heads of the group whipped around toward the entrance. It was Yusuf, who had slipped back into the room unnoticed a minute or two before.

"Well, Yusuf," Lou answered, after resizing him up for a moment, "I would say that yours are."

"Mine?"

"Yes."

"And which claims would mine be?"

Lou instantly regretted the proclamation that left him open to such an easy counter. "Well, I guess I don't know what your individual views are exactly, Yusuf. I was speaking rather of your people's views."

"Oh? And what people would that be?"

"Well, Ishmael's descendants." Lou tried for nonchalance. "The Arab people."

Yusuf nodded. "Another characteristic of conflicts such as these," he said, gesturing toward the board, "is the propensity to demonize others. One way we do this is by lumping others into lifeless categories—by labeling others. We'll talk more about this a little later, but suffice it to say that when we do this, we make masses of unknown people into objects and many of them into our enemies."

"I'm not making anyone into my enemy, Yusuf. I'm merely naming those who have declared me to be their enemy."

"And all Arabs have done this? And they have named you, Lou Herbert, as their enemy?"

At first, Lou was beaten back by this question, but then he leaned back in his chair, a sudden air of rediscovered confidence dancing in his eyes. "Why do you insist on changing the subject?"

"I don't think I have, Lou."

"Oh, yes you have. You keep answering my questions with unrelated questions. The fact is, some parties, small and large, are patently wrong in their beliefs. You don't want to go where my questions are directed, so you create mirages elsewhere."

Yusuf didn't say anything.

"I'll tell you what, Yusuf. I'll answer your questions after you answer mine."

"Fair enough," Yusuf said. "What would you like me to answer?"

# 7 · THE RIGHT THING AND THE RIGHT WAY

"Okay, first of all," Lou began, "I asked whether it makes a difference in a conflict if one side is in the right and the other in the wrong. So I ask you again: doesn't that matter?"

"Yes, it does matter. But not the way you think it does."

"What is that supposed to mean?"

"Well, Lou, have you ever been in a conflict with someone who thought they were wrong?"

Lou thought of Cory and then of the boardroom meeting with his five mutinous executives.

"No," he answered coolly. "But that doesn't mean they're not."

"True," Yusuf said, walking to the front of the room. "But you see, no conflict can be solved so long as all parties are convinced they are right. Solution is possible only when at least one party begins to consider how they might be wrong."

"But what if I'm not wrong?" Lou said.

"If you are not wrong, then you should be willing to consider how you might be mistaken."

"There you go again. What kind of cute riddle is that?"

Yusuf smiled. "It only seems like a riddle, Lou, because we are so unaccustomed to considering the impact of what is below our words, our actions, and our thoughts. There are two ways to seize Jerusalem or to engage in almost any other strategy or behavior, as Avi discussed with you. Which means there is a way I can be wrong even if taking Jerusalem is the best—even the right—thing to do. If I don't remain open to how I might be mistaken in this deeper way, I might live out my life convinced I was on the right side of a given conflict, but I won't have found lasting solutions."

Lou was not convinced and he looked around at the group, searching for an ally.

"The deepest way in which we are right or wrong is in our *way of being* toward others." Yusuf stood beside Avi. "I can be right on the surface—in my behavior or positions—while being entirely mistaken beneath, in my way of being. I might, for example, yell at my kids about the importance of chores and be entirely correct about their importance. However, do you suppose I invite the help and cooperation I am wanting from them when my heart is at war in my yelling and nagging?"

Lou's mind reverted to Cory and to how he had found it difficult to speak a civil word to him for nearly two years.

"So, Lou, in your conflicts with others, even if you are convinced you have been right in the positions you've taken, can you say with confidence that you have also been right in your *way of being* toward them?" Yusuf didn't pause for a response. "Can you say that you have been seeing them as people rather than as objects in your disagreements and that your heart has therefore been at peace rather than at war toward them?"

Lou, still silent, slumped slightly in his chair. He knew that the answer to this question was obvious to everyone in the room. Not only was his heart not at peace toward others, but it seemed to revel in interpersonal warfare.

"We've been asking whether we can see others as people even when we are convinced we are in the right. But think about the reverse for a minute. Have you ever been in the wrong and had someone else see you as a person despite that fact?"

Immediately scenes of a night from Lou's teenage years raced through his memory. He had grown up in Athens, New York, a picturesque town located on the Hudson River 120 miles north of Manhattan and 30 miles south of Albany. His father was an apple farmer who worked around the clock seven days a week to eke out a meager living. They lived in a Civil War–era white clapboard farmhouse that sat only fifty yards off the west bank of the Hudson. Their farm was a rather modest ten acres, but it was the prettiest parcel in Greene County, occupying a peninsula that jutted out into the Hudson. From the top floor of the farmhouse, you could see the Catskill Mountains rising above the trees to the west. The setting was so beautiful that Lou's father could never bring himself to leave, even though he could have run a far grander operation elsewhere.

Through Lou's youth, the family had owned only one vehicle—a red 1942 farm truck with a matching red four-foot-tall wooden bay on the flatbed. The truck rattled and coughed like a ninety-year-old chain-smoker. Lou grew up thinking that the shoulder of the road was merely a second lane, as his father nearly always hugged the grasses that lined the streets to let other vehicles pass.

It was no small thing, then, when the Herberts purchased a new car. Lou was sixteen at the time, and he was eager to show the car to his friends in town. The day after his father brought it home, Lou asked if he could take it for some errands. Sensing his son's excitement, Lou's father readily agreed.

Lou ran out to the driveway and started it up. The low hum of the engine exhilarated him and he stroked the dash in anticipation. Just then he remembered he had left his wallet in the house and ran in to get it. When he raced back out, to his horror, the car had vanished! Lou remembered his feeling of panic and then the awful thought that the car might have rolled down the slope and spilled off the driveway and into the Hudson.

*Didn't I put it back in park?* Lou had screamed in his mind as he ran down the drive. *Didn't I set the brake?*

Where the lane turned, sure enough, fresh tire tracks headed down the hill toward the river. Lou sprinted to the edge of the bluff and looked some twenty feet down. There looking back at him were the headlights of his father's car. He stood frozen as the water slowly sucked the car under the surface and out of sight.

Lou remembered walking numbly up to the house, wondering how he could break the news to his father. He entered the farmhouse and saw his father facing away from him in his favorite wingback chair. He was reading the newspaper. For a moment, Lou considered quietly exiting, and his mind raced with thoughts of running away.

"Forget something else?" his father had asked without turning around.

"No." Lou was cornered. There was no avoiding it now, as his father knew he was in the house. There was nowhere to hide.

"Dad," he had said, his voice breaking. "I…" He couldn't go on. "I…"

He gasped for air and the courage to tell what happened.

"Dad, I…the car…" he stammered as his chest heaved between

words. "I think I must have forgotten to set the brake. It's in the river, Dad. The car is in the river! I'm so sorry." He burst into sobs. "I messed up. I'm so sorry."

What happened next seared itself so deeply into Lou's memory, he was sure that should he ever get Alzheimer's or some similar disease, this would be the last memory to leave him.

He remembered trembling while waiting for his father to respond. His father didn't turn to him but still sat holding the newspaper wide before him. He then slowly reached his left hand to the top corner of the right-hand page and turned it to continue reading. And then he said it, the sentence Lou would never forget. He said, "Well, I guess you'll have to take the truck then."

As Lou remembered this, he sat stunned anew. There had been no retribution, no lecture, no visible anger. Just, "Well, I guess you'll have to take the truck then."

Lou realized in this moment that his father's heart was at peace toward him, a peace so powerful that it couldn't be interrupted even by a provocation so great as the sudden loss of a hard-earned car. Perhaps in his wisdom he knew Lou was now the last person who would ever put another car into the river. Perhaps in that instant he divined that a lecture would serve no purpose and to start one would only hurt an already hurting son.

*An already hurting son.* Lou reeled at the thought. He had one of those too but had rarely spared the lecture. *What have I become?* he wondered silently. *Why do I turn so quickly to war?*

"I'm guessing we've all had that experience, or at least I hope so," Yusuf continued, bringing Lou back to the present. "If you have been seen as a person when you didn't deserve it, then you know that not only is it possible to see others as people when they are in the wrong, but it is the only real way to help them change. To do this requires a heart that is truly at peace."

*That's exactly what Dad had,* Lou thought.

"I've seen him when he's that way, Yusuf," Carol said. "I've seen Lou when his heart is at peace. Many times, actually."

Lou turned to her, his mouth opening slightly in grateful surprise.

"Lou can be warm and helpful—despite what you've seen today." She paused. "Can I share a story?"

"Please." Yusuf nodded.

"Before that, I need to apologize to you, Miguel. It was unkind what I said earlier, about Ria having to do everything. It was inconsiderate and presumptuous of me. I'm sorry. I hope you can forgive me."

Miguel cleared his throat. "No worries." He smiled. "Forgot all about it."

"Thank you. That means a lot to me."

She turned back to the group. "Okay, so the story. This won't be easy for me. I've never shared this with anyone except Lou and one other person I'll tell you about. But I'm thinking it might be helpful for you—for everyone here—to hear this.

"For years in our marriage, I carried a secret." Carol looked down at her lap. "I was bulimic. And I was ashamed about it. I didn't want to let Lou down or to risk losing him or his love. So I never told him. Then something happened that awoke me to the possibility that I might be killing myself—not just emotionally and psychologically but physically as well. I had been severely fatigued for a long time and finally went to see my doctor about it. She ran lots of tests and then asked me point-blank whether I had an eating disorder. At first I denied it. But when she showed me the test results and told me that my body was breaking down and that my health and perhaps even my life were at risk, I finally broke down myself. I told her the truth between sobs."

Lou put his hand on her leg, knowing this was a difficult story to share. This small gesture was not overlooked by anybody in the room.

"But then came the hard part. I knew I had to tell Lou because this problem had morphed way beyond merely a physical ailment." She looked at Lou. "I needed his help, and I couldn't go on keeping such a secret from him daily, even if I didn't need his help. So I told him, deathly worried that it might be the beginning of the end of our marriage."

Lou shook his head, and the emotions associated with this event came flooding back.

"But it wasn't like that. I think he was hurt by the secret keeping, but he didn't dwell on it. At least, not that I know of. His concern for me was immediate and overwhelming. I don't think I've ever been so grateful for anyone in my life as I was for him in that moment and the months that followed. We agreed that I would report to him every night about how I had done during the day. There were many days that I had to report meekly to him that I had stumbled. But stumble or not, he gently rubbed my back until I went to sleep. Somewhere amid the back rubs and his listening to my troubles, my compulsion eventually left me. I haven't even been tempted toward bulimia since that time, which is now many years ago."

As Carol shared her story, the atmosphere in the room began changing. Lou's face, which for much of the morning had been creased with impatience and acrimony, had softened. Carol herself seemed to come alive with a kind of personal conviction and confidence.

"Anyway, I thought it might help to share that story. He's far from perfect," she said with a gentle grin, "but fundamentally he's a good man. That's why I wanted to marry him and why I'm still glad about that, despite the challenge we sometimes are for each other."

Lou hung his head a bit. Some might have thought he had tired of attention that must have seemed too effusive for his taste. In reality, however, he was feeling shame. He remembered well the experience Carol had related, but he knew he too rarely lived up to that ideal.

"Thank you, Carol, for sharing that," Yusuf said.

Carol nodded.

Yusuf turned his attention to the room. "Gwyn, I'm curious. What did hearing that story do for you?"

Gwyn was caught off guard by the question and collected herself for a moment. "I'm not sure what you mean."

"Did it influence your impression of Lou?"

Gwyn paused. "I suppose it did somewhat, yes."

"Elizabeth?" Yusuf asked. "How about you? Did the story do anything for you?"

Elizabeth looked over at Lou for a moment before responding. "Yes, it did."

"What did it do?"

She looked back at Yusuf. "It reminded me of someone." She looked as if she were going to say more, then relaxed into silence.

"So do the two of you now think that Lou was right in everything he has said today?"

"Hell, no," Gwyn said jokingly. "But he's more human to me now."

"Oh, I don't know that I have been thinking Lou has been entirely wrong," Elizabeth said. "I suppose I've been finding him interesting, let's put it that way."

"I'll take it," Lou said.

"How about you, Lou? Do you now think that Gwyn has been right, for example, and that you have been wrong?"

"No, sir." The formality surprised everyone, including Lou.

"But when do you think the two of you would be more able to resolve any differences you might have, right now or thirty minutes ago?"

They glanced quickly at each other. Lou shrugged. "Now, I suppose."

Gwyn nodded in agreement.

"Why is that, do you think?" Yusuf asked. "You still don't agree with the other person's positions, so why do you suppose you'd be more able now than before to find solutions?"

Pettis spoke up. "It's what you and Avi have been talking about: Carol's story humanized Lou, I think. In your words, I think we're seeing others in the room as people more than we might have been before."

"Yes." Yusuf smiled gently. "And that seems to make a difference, doesn't it?"

Pettis and the rest of the group nodded their heads.

"So," Yusuf continued, "if we are going to find lasting solutions to difficult conflicts or external wars we find ourselves in, we first need to find our way out of the internal wars that are poisoning our thoughts, feelings, and attitudes toward others. If we can't put an end to the violence within us, there is no hope for putting an end to the violence without."

"Then how do we end internal violence?" Pettis asked.

Yusuf nodded. "In order to understand how to create peace, we first must understand how and why we have turned toward war. But it's now past lunchtime."

Everyone in the room looked at their watches almost in unison. They were surprised by the time.

"Let's break for lunch and meet back here at 2:00 p.m. Then we'll get into how our hearts have turned from peace to war. Fair enough?"

Everyone nodded.

"One quick thing before you go," Yusuf said. "While you are out, I challenge you to see everyone you encounter as a person—the driver in the car next to you, the person who waits on you at whatever restaurant you go to, your spouse or partner you are with, and so on. Make a point of seeing others over the next ninety minutes as people and see what happens as a result. Fair enough?"

The group, now beginning to stand, nodded.

"Oh, and Teri and Carl," Yusuf called, "can I talk to you for a moment?"

As Lou was leaving the room, he heard Yusuf say to them, "Your daughter, Jenny—"

"Yes?"

"She's running."

# PART II

## FROM PEACE TO WAR

# 8 · REALITY

"Did you hear that, Carol?" Lou said, chasing after her out to the parking lot. "That girl, Jenny—you know, the one who was yelling and carrying on this morning—she took off running."

"Where?"

"Here, out in the streets. She just took off running across town."

Carol stopped. "Oh, how terrible." She looked up the street, one hand shielding her eyes from the noonday sun. "Poor girl. She wasn't wearing any shoes. Do you think we should try to find her?"

"I'm sure Yusuf and his team are handling it."

Before now, Carol would have considered this a sarcastic dig, but she thought she heard a hint of respect in Lou's voice.

Lou glanced at his watch. "Listen, Carol, I have to make some calls."

"Now?"

"Yes. The situation at the office is a mess. I have to check in with a couple of people."

"Can't you do that later?"

"They'll probably be gone home by the time we're out of this... whatever this is. I need to call now."

"You never worried about calling them at home on Friday nights before." She flashed a wry smile. "Why now?"

Lou knew what Carol was searching for, but he didn't want her to have the satisfaction of knowing he was actually considering what Avi and Yusuf had said. "Well, I'd rather not call them at home if I can help it. Not with all the turmoil everyone's in. I need to make things right."

"Okay, Boss. I'll bring you back something to eat."

Lou didn't respond. He was already looking around outside for a private place to make his calls.

There was one person to call first: his assistant. Lou dialed, but the call went straight to her voice mail. *Where is she?* he thought.

"Please leave me a message," came the pleasant voice.

"Susan, it's Lou. Just checking in for a report. I'll try you later." In that moment, he suddenly flashed back to the blustery way he'd left the office the day before and felt a tinge of regret. "Oh, and one more thing. I'm, uh…" he hesitated. "I'm sorry for blowing up at you yesterday on my way out of town. I didn't mean it. I think I was just feeling the load of all that's going on, and I ended up taking it out on you. So, sorry about that. Anyway, that's all. Carry on."

*"Carry on"?* Lou repeated to himself as he hung up the phone. *You can't do any better than that? "Carry on"?* Lou shook his head.

Other than feeling a bit of chagrin over his military-issue good-bye, Lou felt good having made the call to Susan. *This whole "heart at peace" thing might be more intuitive than it sounded.*

But the next call was going to be harder. It was to Kate Stenarude, who had led the mutiny of his executive staff.

Kate had been one of the original twenty employees at Zagrum, where she started as an order fulfillment clerk after graduating from college with a degree in history. It turns out she had been a brilliant hire, as her combination of brains, collaborative spirit, and professional drive quickly elevated her to the top of the sales division. Despite being young, until the March Meltdown, she had been everyone's pick as Lou's successor—if and when he ever decided to retire, that is. This love for her was partly born of desperation, as she was the single person who possessed the business vision and smarts required to run the operation while also retaining a deep appreciation for the people around her, regardless of rank or position. When she walked in the Zagrum doors each morning as one of Zagrum's executives, she walked and talked and greeted and laughed the same as the day she was hired. She walked in not as a big shot but as one of the people. A hard worker. And the people loved her for it.

So when she walked out of the building on that rainy Connecticut March morning, it was as though the company's heart and soul walked out with her. Lou knew this, although until now he had been trying to deny the full impact of her leaving. But the truth was that her loss hurt the company more than the loss of the other four executives combined. And probably more, even, than if Lou had left himself.

He had to call her. *But what am I going to say?* He stood there with the clumsy uncertainty he once felt as a teenager when he was trying to motivate himself to call and ask a girl out.

*Ah, hell. Just call her!* he shouted internally, shaming himself for exhibiting adolescent timidity.

He dialed the number and waited: one ring, then two, three, four.

With each ring he felt the youthful panic build again within him until he was telling himself that if she didn't pick up by ring six, he would hang up.

The sixth ring hadn't even completed before he terminated the call, droplets of sweat forming on his brow. *Well, I tried. I'll catch her later.*

But his racing heart told him that he might not get the courage up to do it again for days. If ever.

His blood pressure was already up: Might as well make use of it. Time for the real work. He dialed up John Rencher, the president of the local union, who was threatening a strike.

"Hello?"

"John." It was more of a summons to attention than a greeting.

"Yes."

"It's Lou Herbert."

Silence. Just then Lou thought of Yusuf's assignment to see everyone as people.

He smiled, trying to manufacture kindness in his voice. "Hey, listen, John, I was wondering if we could get together when I get back and take another look at your proposal."

"Take another look at it yourself. You've had it for a week."

The smile twitched. "I just thought you and I could get further if we talked things over."

"So you still want more from us?" John asked.

"Well, this is a negotiation, after all."

"No, Lou, this is an ultimatum. We're going to shut you down until you meet our demands. You've railroaded our people for too long. It's over, Lou."

"Now you listen here, you little scumbag," Lou exploded. "You wanna go to war with me? Done. But if you walk out on me, you're over at Zagrum. The union will never walk through my doors again. You got that?"

Silence.

"I said, *you got that?*"

But the line was dead. Rencher had hung up.

Lou flung the phone at the wall. "Stupid homework," he muttered. "See people as people." His face twisted with sarcasm. *What a joke,* he thought. *Avi hasn't worked a day in the real world. What's his work experience anyway—Peace Camp?*

*And Yusuf,* he thought, examining the dented corner of his phone. *Try your little soft-heart stuff on the union. Yeah, that'll work. And on the terrorists. And on Cory too. Sure, they'll all just roll over and pant happily after receiving a little of your Middle Eastern love lecture.* He laughed, half out of rage, half out of disgust. *What a waste. This whole thing is a waste.*

"Lou?"

Jolted from his thoughts, he spun round to see Gwyn approaching him. "Do you have a minute?"

"Uh, sure," Lou responded hesitantly.

"I know we've been a bit rough on each other this morning. I'm sorry for that. I didn't want to say anything in the room out of respect for Carol and her story, but I wanted to talk to you about what she shared back there, about her bulimia."

"Okay."

"I work with women with eating disorders. And I know that Carol was sharing her experience to help all of us see you differently, but there were some things she said that troubled me."

When Lou didn't say anything Gwyn hesitantly continued. "I debated all through lunch as to whether I should say anything, but I thought that if I was in your shoes, I'd want to know."

"Yeah, what is it?"

"Eating disorders, they're usually about control. Not always, but often when people don't feel that they have control over their own lives, they can feel a sense of control by at least controlling their own eating. It can be a way to take just a little bit of power back."

"Okay," Lou said again, sensing and bothered by where this was going.

"I think my daughter is here because, well, at least partly because much of her behavior is a reaction to my attempts to control her. I think Carol might feel a lot like Jamie, my daughter. I know the eating disorder is behind Carol, but it seems like the deeper thing might not be."

"And this deeper thing is what?" Lou asked, bristling. "What are you implying?"

"I'm just saying that it might be helpful for you to consider how you see Carol, just like I am trying to consider how I see Jamie. I think people bend to people like us, Lou, but people don't like bending. They resist in lots of ways. Eating disorders can be one way people take control."

"Listen, lady. You don't know me and you don't know Carol. After four hours, you don't know anything about us. So I really don't need your unsolicited diagnosis of our marriage. You heard Carol. She was sharing that experience to get you off my back, and the way we worked through it is a bright spot for us."

"I get that. I really do. And I don't mean to offend you or diagnose you. I just want to help."

"Yeah, thanks for the help," Lou said sarcastically, already turning to go back inside. "And I have lots of women in my company, by the way," he said loudly, not even turning his head over his shoulder. "Lots."

When Carol returned from lunch with a takeout box for Lou in her hand, Lou intercepted her before she could enter the building.

"Carol, we're leaving."

"What?"

"You heard me. We're leaving."

"Leaving?" She laughed sharply. "Why?"

"Because this is a waste of time, and I don't have time to waste."

Carol looked at him warily. "What happened on your calls, Lou?"

"Nothing."

"Seriously, Lou, what happened?"

"Okay, I'll tell you, if you really want to know. I was yanked back to reality, that's what happened. Someone brought me back to my senses. Come on. We're going."

Lou got into the car.

Carol didn't budge.

"Carol," Lou said, rolling down the window. "I said we're leaving."

"I know what you said, but I won't allow it. Not this time, Lou. The stakes are too high."

"You're damn right the stakes are too high, Carol. That's why we have to go."

"No, Lou, that's why we have to stay. The stakes you're worried about, whatever they are, are high because of how we've been mostly tone deaf to what we're starting to learn here. I'm not leaving, Lou."

"Okay, have it your way, Carol." He waved her off with both hands. "I'm leaving then."

Carol stood in silence. The hope that had developed within her through the morning was now fading. *See him as a person, see him as a person. You've got to keep seeing him as a person.*

"Lou."

He put the car back into park and turned to her. "Yeah?"

"If you leave here … if you leave here, honey, I'll leave you."

"You'll what?"

In this moment, Carol was struck by how much she loved this man. Despite his belligerence, she was not raging within toward him. And his bullheadedness did not wash from her memory the many wonderful things he had done for her and for others. He wasn't a saint, to be sure, but there were times—especially during some of the private moments that make up most of life—that he cared and loved and acted in saintly ways. He was better in private than he was in the glare of public moments, which was just the opposite of many people she knew. And it seemed to her that his brand of private strength and public weakness showed more goodness and character than those who hid private weakness with conjured public strength. She'd take him again if they had the chance to do everything over.

So she was surprised when she heard herself say it again. "I'll leave you, Lou. And I mean it."

Lou sat for a moment in complete silence. Every muscle in his body had frozen still, as if afraid to move.

"Carol." His voice was soft, almost pleading. "You can't be serious."

Carol nodded slightly. "Yes, Lou, I'm afraid I am." She sighed. "Don't misunderstand. I don't want to leave you. But I will."

Lou gripped the steering wheel, his knuckles turning white.

"Listen, Lou, I think we need this. I think Cory needs it from us. And I think we need it for him and for each other. You might need it for Zagrum too. And for Kate."

*Kate.* Just the mention of her name took Lou back into the feeling he had when he knew he needed to call her. That seemed like years ago.

He heaved a heavy sigh.

"Okay, Carol. You win. I'll stay." The car's hum died as he took out the key. "But only until tonight."

# 9 • THE BEGINNING OF AN IDEA

Lou picked at the soggy deli sandwich Carol had brought him while the group assembled back in the room. Apart from tension between Gwyn and Lou, the mood was much lighter among the group than it had been at the beginning when they were sizing each other up. Carl was deep in conversation with Miguel. Elizabeth and Carol were in the back of the room browsing a Camp Moriah leaflet together.

Just then, Pettis walked up to Lou from behind.

"So, Lou," he said, as if they were picking up a prior conversation, "four years in 'Nam."

Lou nodded, wondering if Gwyn had already talked to Pettis about their latest interchange.

"Hats off to you, my friend," Pettis continued, seemingly unaware. "I was there, but it's different flying above the jungle than it was down below. I know that."

Lou nodded appreciatively. In peacetime, pilots always think themselves superior to the so-called grunts on the ground. And the infantrymen carry around an inferiority complex about it as well, although they'd never admit it. In wartime, however, the psychology changes. The high-flying pilots quickly develop a deep admiration for their partners on the ground. And soldiers on the ground, although grateful for their cover when they hear the roar of supportive aircraft overhead, would tell you, if pressed, that those well-heeled flyboys never get their uniforms dirty enough or their vital parts close enough to the crosshairs of the enemy to know real bravery—or fear, for that matter. In Vietnam and elsewhere, the grunts receive the lion's share of the admiration and respect of fellow soldiers. But Lou also knew there were very few African Americans who served as pilots in Vietnam. He could only guess at the tenacity and grit that would be required of any African Americans to fight their way to the cockpit during that time.

"Thanks, Pettis. It's good to be with a fellow vet." Lou gave him an approving nod. "Tell me, what is it you do in Texas?"

Avi and Yusuf walked in the room, and Pettis patted Lou on the shoulder before returning to his seat, along with most of the group. Lou looked across at Jenny's parents, who appeared to be okay, a surprise to him under the circumstances.

"Well, welcome back," Avi greeted them. "Before we move forward, does anyone have any questions about anything?"

Lou shot his hand up—the first time he hadn't just blurted out a comment. "What happened to Jenny?"

"Jenny is fine," Yusuf said. "As some of you may know, she took off running soon after we started this morning."

"Have you caught her?" Lou asked.

"Actually, Lou, we're not trying to catch her," Yusuf said. "This is a voluntary program, so we won't force anyone into it. But we will make sure she stays safe. And we'll do that in a way that invites her, as much as possible, to choose to join with us."

Lou was perplexed. "So what does that mean you're doing?"

"It means two of our staff are following her, trying to engage her in conversation, and a truck with backup if needed is following behind but out of sight. Everything will be fine." He smiled. "Anything else?"

Lou raised his hand again.

"This whole 'see people as people or see them as objects' distinction, where does it come from?"

Avi spoke first. "It really is at the heart of our experience as human beings with each other." He paused as Elizabeth found her seat. "And understanding our experience as human beings has been at the heart of what philosophers have tried to understand for a long time. Perhaps it would help to give a brief overview." He looked over at Yusuf, who nodded.

Avi turned back to the group. "I hesitate talking philosophy with you." He smirked apologetically. "Especially first thing after lunch. But I'll take a chance on it, for a minute or two anyway. If you're pretty sure you don't want any philosophy, just plug your ears for a minute." He looked around the room. "You are all familiar with the philosopher René Descartes?"

"Not a bad philosopher—for a Frenchman," Elizabeth cracked. Her hands were no longer clasped together, and she was leaning back comfortably in her chair.

"Not bad indeed," Avi grinned. "Descartes is the father of what is known as the modern period of philosophy, and he is famous still to this day for the starting point of his very ambitious philosophical theory, which he hoped would explain all of existence. His foundational assumption was the famous line *Cogito, ergo sum—* or, 'I think, therefore I am.'

"But you will notice there are big assumptions in Descartes's starting point," Avi continued. "The biggest of these is the assumption of the primacy of the separate human consciousness—what Descartes called the *I*.

"Hundreds of years after Descartes, a series of philosophers began to call into question the modern philosophical arguments that Descartes started in motion, in particular this central individualistic assumption that undergirded Descartes's work. If one of these philosophers had been a contemporary of Descartes, he might have asked him this question: 'René, tell me—from where did you acquire the language that enabled you to formulate the thought "I think, therefore I am"?'"

Avi looked around the group to let that question settle on them. "Of course, Descartes acquired those words, and the ability to think with them, from others. Which is to say, he did not conjure them as a separate, individualized I."

Lou eyed the coffee at the refreshments table.

"Consider what this means for Descartes's theory," Avi continued. "There is a kind of brute fact that just is—the fact of *being in the world with others*. Descartes was able to postulate that the separate self was what was most fundamental only because he acquired language in a world *with others*."

"Ah," Elizabeth said, "so being in the world with others, and not the idea of a separate self, is what is fundamental. Is that what you are suggesting?"

"Exactly," Avi agreed. "Descartes's foundational assumption is disproved by the conditions that made it possible for him to state it in the first place. That is why many subsequent philosophers, with their dismantling of individualism, shifted their focus away from the separate self and onto our being with others.

"One of these philosophers was Martin Buber, whom I mentioned this morning. He asserted that our way of being in the world is what is most fundamental to human experience. He observed that there are basically two ways of being in the world: we can be in the world seeing others as people, or we can be in the world seeing others as objects. He called the first way of being the I-Thou way and the second the I-It way, and he argued that we are always, in every moment, being either I-Thou or I-It—seeing others as people or seeing others as objects.

"So, Lou," he said, turning to face him, "that is a long way of saying that it was Martin Buber who first observed these two basic ways of being, or at least formulated them that way. He was the first to articulate the differences in human experience when we are seeing others as objects as opposed to seeing them as they are, as people." He looked around at the rest of the group. "Okay, it's safe to unplug your ears now."

"Well, almost," Yusuf interjected with a smile. "Let me add one more thought. Buber's observation of these two ways of being raised the question of how we move from one way of being to another—from seeing people as people, for example, to seeing others as objects and vice versa. But this is a question Buber never answered. He simply observed the two ways of being and their differences. It is left to us, now, to figure out how we can change our way of being—if we want to, that is."

Yusuf smiled thoughtfully. "For our purposes, the question Buber did not address is the question we must answer. We have been suggesting that the foundational problem in our homes, our workplaces, and our battlefields is that our hearts are too often at war—that is, we too often insist on seeing people as objects. And we have seen how one warring heart invites more 'object seeing' and war in others. It follows from this that in order to find peace, we must first understand how we and others have foregone peace and chosen war."

"Sometimes we don't choose war," Lou said. "It chooses us."

"Yes, Lou," Yusuf agreed. "Sometimes we might be forced to defend ourselves, you're exactly right. But that is a different thing than saying that we are forced to despise, to rage, to denigrate, to belittle. No one can force a warring heart upon us. When our hearts go to war, we ourselves have chosen it."

"How?" Lou asked.

"That is exactly what we will now explore," Yusuf said.

# 10 • CHOOSING WAR

"I was raised," Yusuf began, "in a village of rock-walled homes in the hills on the western edge of Jerusalem. The village, called Deir Yassin, had been my family's home for at least two centuries. But that all ended early on the morning of April 9, 1948, during the Arab-Jewish fighting surrounding the establishment of Israel. I was just five years old at the time. I remember being awakened by shouting and gunfire. Our village was being attacked by what I later learned were members of a Jewish underground military group. My father grabbed me from bed and pushed me and my two sisters into my parents' room. He then pulled a rifle from under his mattress and, pulling on his boots, ran out of the house. 'Stay inside!' he yelled to us. 'Don't come out for anyone, you hear? Until I return, God willing.'

"Those were the last words I ever heard my father speak. When it was over and we left the protection of our stone walls, bodies and exploded body parts littered the streets. My father was among the dead."

"How terrible," Ria said.

"It was many years ago." Yusuf paused. "Those days and the years that followed were difficult for me and my family, I won't deny it. But we weren't the only ones that suffered tragedy."

Elizabeth spoke up. "I was going to say, I have some Jewish friends that have similar stories to tell."

"I'm sure you do," Yusuf said, "as do I. A Jewish village called Kfar Etzion was attacked by Arab forces at around the same time, for example. The village was basically massacred, so I can hardly say that my fate was worse than theirs. By telling my story, I did not mean to imply that Arabs are the only ones that have suffered unjustly. I'm sorry if it seemed that way. Avi's father, for example, was killed while defending his country against an Arab attack. That hurt him as much as losing my father hurt me. Over the years and centuries, violence has been hurled hatefully in all directions. That is the tragic, bloody truth."

Lou was glad to hear Yusuf own up to what he felt were Arab atrocities, but he was uneasy all the same. It seemed to Lou that Yusuf was too quick to equate Arab and Israeli suffering when in Lou's mind the scales of unjustified suffering clearly leaned in the Israeli direction. Lou wasn't sure, but he thought he might have an ally in this belief in Elizabeth Wingfield.

"After my father died," Yusuf continued, "my mother moved us to the M'askar refugee camp in the Old City of Jerusalem. I was eight years old. Because my mother was only able to make a small living, I would spend most of each day in front of the Old City's Christian holy sites as a street hustler. My job was to make the Westerners who came on pilgrimages feel sorry for me and then lead them to the shops of the people who had hired me. In broken English, I began to interact with the West.

"As for the Jews, I had little opportunity or desire to inter-act with them. As a result of the 1948 war, Jordan took control of the West Bank and East Jerusalem, including the Old City, and all the Jews who had been there fled to what became Israel.

Border penetrations from both directions, whether for military or economic reasons, usually ended in gunfire and casualties. The Jews were our enemies."

Lou looked at Avi, who was looking at the blue marker in his hands.

"At least," Yusuf said, "this is the simplistic picture most often recited and remembered. The truth was a bit more nuanced. I know because I worked the same Old City streets as a certain elderly Jewish man. This man lived in Israeli West Jerusalem and, as dangerous as it now seems in retrospect, would sneak over the border to the Old City in Jordanian-controlled East Jerusalem— the place where most of the pilgrimage sites are located that are frequented by wealthy Western tourists—to beg for money outside the Church of the Holy Sepulchre. The war had severely reduced the number of foreign visitors, so merchants were hard up for customers, appealing to the same Western wallets for the same Western money.

"Which brings me to the story I want to share with you. I had come to know this man, Mordechai Lavon, at what you might call a close distance. We often worked the streets within mere feet of each other, and although I was well acquainted with his voice and he with mine, I had never once addressed him, even though he tried to strike up a conversation on occasion.

"One day, he stumbled as he asked a passerby for help. His purse burst open as it hit the ground, and his coins flew in all directions into the street.

"As he groped first for his purse and then for his scattered coins, I had a sudden thought. You might call it a sense of something to do—something I knew in that instant was the right thing to do. I think it would be accurate, in fact, to call it a desire. That is, I felt a desire to help him—first to help him to his feet and then to retrieve his coins for him.

"I had a choice, of course. I could act on this sense I had, or I could resist it. Which do you suppose I did?"

"I'd imagine you helped," Carol said.

"No, he didn't." Lou smirked. "He wouldn't be telling the story if he had."

Yusuf smiled. "True enough, Lou. You're right. I resisted the sense I had to help Mordechai. A stronger way to say it is that I betrayed that sense and acted contrary to what I knew was right in that moment. Instead of helping, I turned and walked the other way."

Lou gave a self-satisfied smile.

"As I was walking away," Yusuf said, "what sorts of things do you suppose I might have started to say and think to myself about Mordechai Lavon?"

"That he was a competitor," Carl responded. "As you said, there is only so much Western money to go around."

"That he shouldn't have been there anyway," Gwyn said. "You and the rest of your neighbors were kind to allow him to sneak over to Arab territory to beg. After all, he was part of the enemy who robbed you of your peace. A Zionist threat. A bigot."

As Gwyn talked, Yusuf wrote these statements on the board.

"This might seem strange," Ria added, "given that we all would hope to have pity on an elderly beggar. But I could also imagine that you could feel disgust."

"Interesting," Yusuf said. "Say more about that."

"Well, even though you were a beggar, he was an old beggar. I am guessing that you hoped that you wouldn't be doing this for life, but here was a man who ended as a beggar, not someone who started as one."

"That is exactly how I felt," Yusuf said. "Isn't it remarkable that even though you haven't had my life experience, what you just shared was exactly how I felt? I saw Mordechai as a competitor, as a threat, and I felt disgust for just the reasons you described. You see, even though our life experiences are very different, we all know firsthand the experience of looking for and finding justification for our mistreatment of others. We're all very skilled at it."

"Okay then," Yusuf continued, "if I was starting to see Mordechai in these ways we've mentioned, how do you suppose I might have started to see myself?"

"As a victim," Teri answered.

"And as better than he was," Gwyn said.

"I don't know." Carol spoke slowly. "You might have gotten down on yourself—like you weren't good enough. Deep down, I think you would have felt like you weren't being a very good person."

"Maybe so," Gwyn said, "but it wasn't his fault, after everything that had happened. If he was bad, it was because of what others had done to him."

"That sounds like a cop-out," Lou said.

"We'll get to whether it's a cop-out," Yusuf said. "But I think what Gwyn said certainly describes what I was at least believing to be the case at the time."

"Okay." Lou shrugged.

"I'm thinking about how you walked away after you noticed the coins," Teri said. "On the one hand, I can see how a feeling of victimization would invite you to walk away. But I think there could have been another motivation as well."

"Go on," Yusuf invited.

"Well," Teri continued, "I'm thinking that by turning quickly away, you were giving yourself an excuse. Your turn away might have been out of a need to be seen as a good person."

"What do you mean?" Lou asked. "If he turned away, how does that make him a good person?"

"It doesn't," Teri said. "But it makes it easier for him to *claim* that he is. If he didn't need to be seen as being good, he could have just stood and watched Mordechai struggle. But by quickly turning away so it seemed like he didn't see the situation, he preserved his reputation—his claim of goodness."

Yusuf started to chuckle. "That's a really interesting insight, Teri. It reminds me of something that happened just this morning. I was making myself a sandwich, and I noticed that I'd dropped a piece of lettuce on the floor. It would have been easy to bend over and pick it up, but I didn't. Instead, I pushed it under the counter with my toe! I wouldn't have had to do that unless I was concerned with showing my wife, Lina, that I was a good person—tidy, responsible, and so on. Otherwise, I might have just left it there."

"Well, why not just pick it up?" Gwyn laughed. "Honestly!"

"Yes," Yusuf agreed. "And why not just pick up the coins too? That's exactly the question we're beginning to explore."

At that he added "Need to be seen as a good person" to the list he was constructing on the board.

"Okay then," he said, turning back to the group. "When I'm seeing this man and myself in the ways we've discussed, how do you suppose I might have viewed the circumstances I found myself in?"

"As unfair," Gwyn said.

Yusuf started writing that on the board.

"And unjust," added Ria.

"And burdensome," said Pettis. "Given all you'd suffered, I can imagine you went around feeling angry or depressed."

"Yes," Elizabeth said. "In fact, you might have felt that the whole world was lined up against you—against your happiness, against your security, against your well-being."

"Excellent. Thank you." Yusuf finished writing. "Now, I'd like to play off something Pettis just said—that I might have felt angry or depressed. Can you think of any other ways I might have felt given the way I was seeing everything else?"

"You would have been bitter," Gwyn said.

"Okay, excellent," Yusuf said, adding "Bitter" to "Angry" and "Depressed" on the diagram. "But if you were to ask me why I was feeling those ways, what do you think I would have said?"

"That it wasn't your fault," Pettis said. "You would have said it was the Israelis' fault—that you felt that way only because of what they had done to you and your people."

Yusuf nodded. "Which is to say that I felt justified in my anger, my depression, and my bitterness. I felt justified in my judgmental view of Mordechai."

Yusuf added the word "Justified" to the diagram. "That's what my entire experience here was telling me," he said, pointing at the board.

"We call the experience of living in this distorted reality being 'in the box,' because when we betray ourselves, we feel trapped by emotions and perceptions of ourselves, others, and the world that aren't true but are very, very convincing." As Yusuf spoke, he drew a box around these distorted views of himself and Mordechai, as well as the feelings and view of the world that he had detailed on the board.

| VIEW OF MYSELF | VIEW OF MORDECHAI |
|---|---|
| Better than | Competitor |
| A victim (so owed) | No right to be there |
| Bad (but made to be) | Robs me of peace |
| Need to be seen as a | Zionist threat |
| good person | Bigot |
| **FEELINGS** | **VIEW OF WORLD** |
| Angry | Unfair |
| Depressed | Unjust |
| Bitter | Burdensome |
| Justified | Against me |

"So you can see," Yusuf continued, "that in the box my whole experience is telling me that I didn't do anything wrong and that others were to blame. That is what I was believing, was it not?"

"Probably," Pettis said. Mumbled agreement spread around the room.

"That I wasn't responsible for how I was seeing and feeling?" Yusuf said.

"Yes."

"But is that true?" Yusuf asked. "Was I really caused by outside forces to see and feel in these ways—the ways I believed when I was in this box? Or was I rather choosing to see and feel in these ways?"

"You're suggesting you were actually choosing to be angry, depressed, and bitter?" Gwyn frowned and folded her arms.

"I'm suggesting I was making a choice that resulted in my feeling angry, depressed, and bitter. A choice that was my choice and no one else's—not Mordechai's, not the Israelis."

Yusuf looked around at a roomful of perplexed faces. "Perhaps it would help," he said, "to put the diagram in context." He then added to the diagram:

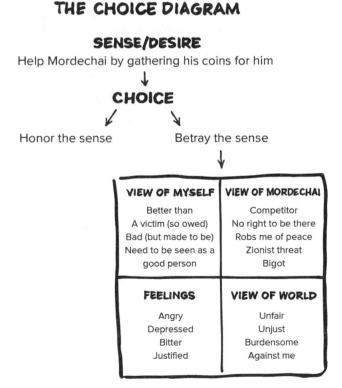

## THE CHOICE DIAGRAM

### SENSE/DESIRE
Help Mordechai by gathering his coins for him

↓

### CHOICE

↙        ↘

Honor the sense        Betray the sense

↓

| VIEW OF MYSELF | VIEW OF MORDECHAI |
|---|---|
| Better than | Competitor |
| A victim (so owed) | No right to be there |
| Bad (but made to be) | Robs me of peace |
| Need to be seen as a | Zionist threat |
| good person | Bigot |
| **FEELINGS** | **VIEW OF WORLD** |
| Angry | Unfair |
| Depressed | Unjust |
| Bitter | Burdensome |
| Justified | Against me |

"As you'll recall," he said, "I had a sense or desire to help Mordechai. I knew it was the right thing to do. But this then presented a choice: I could either honor my sense to help or I could betray it and choose not to help. Which is to say that we don't always do what we know is the right thing to do, do we?"

The group looked uncertain.

"For example," Yusuf continued, "we don't always apologize when we know we should, do we?"

Lou thought of the apology he still owed Kate.

"When a spouse or child or neighbor is struggling with something we could easily help with, we don't always offer that help. And don't we sometimes hold on to information we know we should share with others? At work, for example, when we know a piece of information would help a coworker, don't we sometimes hold it for ourselves?"

Most in the group nodded their heads, including Lou, who knew this scenario well.

"When I choose to act contrary to my own sense of what is appropriate," Yusuf said, "I commit what we at Camp Moriah call an act of self-betrayal. It is a betrayal of my own sense of the right way to act in a given moment in time—not someone else's sense or standard, but what I myself feel is right in the moment.

"Acts of self-betrayal such as those I've mentioned are so common they are almost ho-hum. But when we dig a little deeper, we discover something fascinating about self-betrayal."

He looked around at the group. "A choice to betray myself," he said, "is a choice to go to war."

## 11 · A NEED FOR WAR

"How is a choice to betray oneself a choice to go to war?" There was heaviness in Lou's voice.

"Because when I betray myself," Yusuf said, "I create within myself a new need—a need that causes me to see others accusingly, a need that causes me to care about something other than truth and solutions, and a need that invites others to do the same in response."

"What need is that?" Pettis asked.

Yusuf turned back to the Choice Diagram. "At the beginning here, when I had the desire to help Mordechai, how would you say I was seeing him? Was he a person or an object to me?"

The group gave a collective murmur: "He was a person."

"How about down here at the end, when I was in this box? Was he still a person to me then?"

They looked at the diagram.

Pettis shifted in his seat. "No, you'd dehumanized him. He's almost a caricature."

"So what was he to me at that point, a person or an object?"

"An object," Pettis said.

"Which gives rise to what need?" Yusuf asked.

Pettis and the others puzzled over that. "I'm not sure what you mean," he said.

"Perhaps an analogy would help," Yusuf said. "My father was a carpenter. When I was four or five, I remember going with him on a job where he was helping to rebuild a house. I remember in particular a wall in the kitchen area of the home. It turned out that the wall was crooked. I remember this because of something my father taught me about it. 'Here, Yusuf,' I remember him saying, although in Arabic, of course, 'we need to justify this wall. When something is crooked and we need to make it straight, we call it justifying. This wall is crooked, so it needs to be justified.'"

With that, Yusuf looked around at the group.

"With that analogy in mind," he said, "take another look at the diagram."

Carol's quiet voice came in immediate reply. "You needed to be justified in the story," she said. "That's the need you're talking about, isn't it?"

"Yes, Carol." Yusuf smiled. "It is. And did I have any need to be justified when I had the desire to help Mordechai?"

"No."

"Why not?"

"Because you weren't being crooked toward him in that moment."

"Exactly." Yusuf's face brightened. "Did everyone catch that?" he asked the group.

Heads nodded around the room but they weren't convincing enough.

"Let's be really clear on this," Yusuf said. "What was crooked when I turned my back on Mordechai that wasn't crooked before?"

"Your view of him," Carol said.

"Yes," Yusuf said. "And what was crooked about that view of him?"

"You weren't seeing him as a person any longer," Pettis said. "He didn't count any more. At least not like you counted."

"Exactly. In fact, it was precisely *because* I was seeing him as a person at the beginning of the story that I wanted to help him. But the moment I began to violate the basic call of his humanity upon me, I created within me a new need, a need that didn't exist the moment before; I needed to be justified for violating the truth I knew in that moment—that he was as human and legitimate as I was."

Yusuf paced slightly as he spoke. "Having violated this truth, my entire perception now raced to make me justified. Think about it. When do you suppose Mordechai's personal quirks, whatever they might have been, seemed larger to me, before I betrayed my sense to help him, or after?"

"After," the group answered.

"And when do you suppose the Israelis, the group I lumped Mordechai in with, seemed worse to me? In the moment I had the sense to help Mordechai or after I failed to help him?"

"After," the group repeated.

"So notice," Yusuf continued, "when I betray myself, others' faults become immediately inflated in my heart and mind. I begin to 'horribilize' others. That is, I begin to make them out to be worse than they really are. And I do this because the worse they are, the more justified I feel. A needy man on the street suddenly represents a threat not just to my livelihood but also to my very peace and freedom. A person to help becomes an object to blame."

Yusuf turned to the board and added to the diagram. As he was finishing, Gwyn asked, "But what if Mordechai really was a problem? What if he wasn't some gentle old man but an out-and-out racist jerk? What if he outwardly agreed with the people who had thrust your family from your home? Wouldn't you be justified in that case?"

"What need would I have to be justified if I wasn't somehow crooked?" Yusuf turned from the board to face the group.

Gwyn was clearly frustrated by that answer. "I'm sorry, Yusuf, but I don't know if I can accept that. It seems like you're just giving bad people a pass."

Yusuf's eyes seemed to soften at this comment. "I appreciate how seriously you are grappling with this, Gwyn," he said. Being reflexively cynical himself, he appreciated those who listened with a healthy dose of careful skepticism. "You are worried that I might not be holding people accountable for wrongs they've committed. Am I right?"

"Yes, that's exactly what I mean."

"That's an important issue," Yusuf said. "And I'm guessing that Gwyn isn't the only one with this worry."

Nearly everyone gestured agreement.

"Everyone here is carrying something. You might have suffered some terrible mistreatments at others' hands. All of you as parents here, for example, have undoubtedly been treated terribly at times—unjustly, unfairly, ungratefully. Right?" He looked thoughtfully around the semicircle.

Heads nodded.

"And you may have been railroaded at work as well—blamed, overlooked, unappreciated. Or perhaps you have been mistreated by society generally. Maybe you belong to a religion that is treated prejudicially, or to an ethnic group or race that is systematically marginalized, or to a class that is ignored or despised. I know a thing or two about these mistreatments. I know what they feel like, and I know how terrible they are. I can say from experience that there are few things so painful as contempt from others."

The nods continued.

"Few things except one." Yusuf rested his hands in his pockets. "As painful as it is to receive contempt from another, it is more debilitating by far to be filled with contempt for another. In this too I speak from painful experience. My own contempt for others is the most debilitating pain of all, for when I am in the middle of it—when I'm seeing resentfully and disdainfully—I condemn myself to living in a disdained, resented world."

Yusuf stood still and faced the group. "The reality is, when our hearts are at war, we think that we will be giving others a pass if we choose to see them as people. But this is the distorted think-ing we all experience when we are in the box. The truth is that seeing others as people doesn't require that I turn a blind eye to their behavior and doesn't absolve them of the wrongs they have done. In fact, it is just the opposite. If I refuse to see others as people because of the wrongs they've committed, I give them all the reason they need to not see me and to continue to feel justified in the choices they've made to mistreat me. My mistreatment of them in choosing to not see their humanity becomes their excuse for their ongoing mistreatment of me. In essence, choosing to see them as objects lets them off the hook. So as counterintuitive as it might seem when we are in the box, it is only in choosing to see the humanity of others that we require them to be accountable."

Teri spoke up: "I think I know what you mean. I've seen this in my relationship with Jenny. I have felt mistreated by her so many times, and I felt that she was damaging our family. But when I see her as a problem, she immediately becomes defensive, and she blames her acting out on me. But there have also been moments when I don't see her as a problem—times when I really see her. Not that I don't see her struggles and the problems she is creating for herself and our family. I don't minimize or ignore or excuse any of that. But in those moments she's a person to me. And in those moments when I see her as a person, she doesn't resist me. She softens and has even apologized."

"That's it," Yusuf agreed. "Seeing others as people, regardless of their behavior, is the only thing that invites real accountability."

"But how do you keep yourself from feeling so bothered?" Lou was thinking about the constant tension with his own son. "I get so frustrated with Cory and his behavior and his refusal to be accountable that I can't see Cory as a person most of the time."

"There is a question I have learned to ask myself when I am feeling bothered about others," Yusuf said. "Am I holding myself to the same standard I am demanding of them? In other words, if I am worried that others are getting a pass, am I also worried about whether I am giving myself one? Am I as vigilant in demanding that others be aware of their impact on me as I am in demanding that I stay aware of my impact on them?"

He paused a moment to let that settle.

"If I'm not, I will be living in a kind of fog that obscures all the reality around and within me. Like a pilot in a cloud bank whose senses are telling her just the opposite of what her instrument panel is saying, my senses will be systematically lying to me—about myself, about others, and about my circumstances.

"So, Gwyn, let's come back to your question. What if Mordechai really is a racist jerk? If I mistreat him because he is a racist jerk, where does that leave us? Do I invite him to be accountable for his racism by refusing to see him as a person?"

Gwyn was thinking and didn't respond for a few moments. "You're saying that the only way I invite him to be accountable is if I don't give him the excuse he is looking for that makes his being a jerk okay?" It was more of a statement than a question. "And the excuse I give him to continue to be a jerk is in my mistreatment of him?"

"I think that's right," Yusuf said. "And that mistreatment isn't found just in what I do. That mistreatment is in how I see and regard him."

"But it is hard to see a racist as a person," Gwyn responded.

"Yes, Gwyn, it is. And I want to be really clear here. Nothing we are talking about excuses racism. Racism is evil, as is every other twisted way we dehumanize each other. I should know. I've had to come to terms with my own racism—in some ways inherited, like it is for most people, but I've had to stare it down in the end nonetheless. Nothing excuses racism. Nothing. As an Arab in this country, I also know what it is like when others see me in dehumanizing, demeaning ways. Seeing a racist person as a person doesn't mean I condone their racism. It doesn't even mean that I turn a blind eye to it. But I do see the potential for change; I can see that, like me, this person isn't just a racist. In fact, labeling a person as a racist keeps me from seeing them fully as a person. It reduces them to a single label. But everyone who could be labeled a racist is more than that one word describes. Much more. Everyone has the possibility to get better. But I don't see that when my heart is at war, and I don't want to see it."

"I've never thought about it quite that way," Gwyn said. "This is a hard one for me, but that's helpful."

"Let's think about this in light of my experience with Mordechai. In my story, when would I be more motivated to see Mordechai as a racist? When I felt a sense to help him or after I betrayed my sense?"

"After," Miguel said.

"And why?" Yusuf asked.

Miguel was leaning forward now. "Because if he's a racist then you are justified in how you responded."

"At least I *feel* justified," Yusuf said, smiling.

"Right," Miguel said.

"Notice that I first had the sense to help Morchechai *because* I saw him as a person," Yusuf continued. "Was I filled with resentment or contempt when I first had this sense?"

The group followed Yusuf's gaze back to the diagram.

"No," Ria said.

"But how about at the end of the story," Yusuf asked, "when I was down in this box seeing him as a threat and as unworthy of my help? Was I feeling resentful then?"

The group looked at the feelings that were listed in the box: angry, depressed, bitter, justified. The room nodded. "Yes."

"So why was I feeling that way?" Yusuf asked. "I had certainly suffered my share of hardships. Was that the cause of my bitterness, my anger, my resentment, and my contempt?"

"Probably," Miguel said.

"Look at the diagram again," Yusuf said.

# THE CHOICE DIAGRAM

## SENSE/DESIRE

**Help Mordechai by gathering his coins for him**

(I'm seeing Mordechai as a PERSON with needs,
cares, worries, and fears that matter, like mine do)

**My Heart Is at Peace**

↓

## CHOICE

↙          ↘

Honor the sense          Betray the sense

↓          ↓

I continue to see
Mordechai as a
person like myself

I begin to see
Mordechai in ways that
justify my self-betrayal;
he becomes an OBJECT
I blame

**My Heart Goes to War**

| VIEW OF MYSELF | VIEW OF MORDECHAI |
|---|---|
| Better than | Competitor |
| A victim (so owed) | No right to be there |
| Bad (but made to be) | Robs me of peace |
| Need to be seen as a | Zionist threat |
| good person | Bigot |
| **FEELINGS** | **VIEW OF WORLD** |
| Angry | Unfair |
| Depressed | Unjust |
| Bitter | Burdensome |
| Justified | Against me |

Pettis leaned forward. "No. I'd say your hardships did not cause your feelings."

"Why do you say that?" Yusuf asked.

"Because whatever hardships you had suffered you had already suffered at the beginning of this story. But those hardships didn't prevent you from seeing Mordechai as a person when you felt the desire to help him gather up his coins."

"Exactly," Yusuf said. "So what's the only thing that happened between the time at the beginning of this story when I wasn't feeling angry and bitter and the time at the end when I was? What's the only thing that happened between the time that I saw Mordechai as a person and the time I saw him as an object?"

"Your choice to betray yourself," Pettis said.

"So what was the cause of my anger, my bitterness, my resentment, my contempt, my lack of peace? Was it Mordechai? Or was it me?"

"Well, the diagram says it was you," Lou said.

"But you're not convinced."

"No, I'm not sure that I am." Lou frowned at the cup of cold coffee in his hand. "Look, isn't it possible you simply had a momentary lapse of memory when the coins spilled from Mordechai's purse, a moment when your hardships weren't foremost on your mind? It seems to me that's what likely happened. And then a moment later you came back to reality and remembered all the trouble you'd suffered at the hands of the Israelis. It's not like your bitterness just started in this moment. You'd felt it before. And you might have felt it, like Gwyn said, because of what the Israelis had done to you and your family."

"What, you're siding with me now?" Gwyn grinned.

Lou smirked back. "I know. It has me worried too."

"That's a great question, Lou," Yusuf said. "You're right, of course, that this wasn't the first time I had felt angry and bitter toward the Israelis. And you are right as well in pointing out that my father's death, and the hardships it caused my family, certainly played a role. But I believe it played a role different from the one you are suggesting. You seem to be saying that I ended up feeling the way I did about Mordechai because of what his people had done to me and my family. In other words, the hardships I had suffered *caused* the feelings I came to have about Mordechai. Is that what you are suggesting?"

"It's what I'm wondering, anyway. Yes."

"And I'm proposing something entirely different," Yusuf said. "I'm suggesting that my feelings about Mordechai were not caused by something others had done to me but by something I was doing to Mordechai. They were the result of a choice I was making relative to Mordechai. So how shall we evaluate these very different ways of understanding what was happening?" He looked around at the group.

"I don't know about evaluating them," Elizabeth said, "but Lou's way of seeing this leads to a pretty depressing outcome."

"Which is what?" Yusuf asked.

"That we're all just victims, powerless in the face of difficulty, inevitably doomed to be bitter and angry."

Lou grimaced. "I'm not saying that."

"I think you are," Elizabeth said. "You said the only reason Yusuf wasn't bitter at the beginning of the story was because he simply wasn't thinking about his hardships for a moment. Remembering them caused him to feel bitter and angry again. If that doesn't make one powerless in the face of hardship, I don't know what does."

Lou had to admit she had a point. He didn't believe in that kind of helpless victimhood either. He knew of too many great souls who had passed through terrible mistreatment without becoming embittered by it to believe that mistreatment left us without choices. But it does have an impact, doesn't it? He was thinking of Cory.

"Excellent points, Elizabeth," Yusuf said. "I'd like to continue with your idea." Yusuf inhaled slowly. "Not having a memory at the forefront of my mind is different than having forgotten it. I can assure you that there has never been a moment in my life since my father's death that I haven't remembered that he died and how he died. Having said that, Lou is right that the level and nature of my focus is often very different from moment to moment. Lou reasoned that this fact allowed me to see Mordechai differently in the moment I had the inclination to help him. Actually, however, Lou's theory has it exactly backwards. It isn't that I saw Mordechai as a person because I wasn't dwelling on my hardships. Rather, it was that I wasn't dwelling on my hardships because I was seeing Mordechai as a person. I needed to dwell on my hardships only when I needed to be justified for treating Mordechai poorly. My hardships were my excuse at that point. When I didn't need an excuse, I was free not to dwell on them."

"Oh, so an abused woman is at fault for the pain caused by her abuser?" Gwyn gave a frustrated sigh. "I'm sorry if I can't go there."

Yusuf paused and took in a deep breath. "I couldn't go there either, Gwyn," he said. "But may I share a story with you?"

Yusuf took a piece of paper out of a folder on a table in the front corner of the room. "This is from a letter I received in the mail a few years ago," he said. "It was written by one of our former students here who had fallen on very difficult times in her marriage. Rather than try to give you the context for it, I will let her speak for herself."

He began reading:

> *One Friday more than a year ago, my estranged husband came to visit me at my parents' home. He came over relatively frequently, presumably to visit our daughter but really to try to win me back. Shortly before he left on this particular day, he asked me to show him a copy of our life insurance policy. He asked if we were paid up on it and asked me to double-check his reading of a phrase in the suicide clause. By the time I closed the door behind him that evening, his intentions were obvious. David was going to commit suicide. I said good-bye, expecting that I would never see my husband alive again.*
>
> *I could hardly contain my excitement.*
>
> *You see, my charming young groom had become violent shortly after our marriage. Within months, I had grown so terrified of him that I would not do anything, even turn on the television, without his approval. He was extremely jealous and soon forced me to throw away my address book, my high school yearbooks, and even pictures of my family. He threatened my life, humiliated*

*me in public, flirted openly with other women, and finally reduced even our physical intimacy to violence.*

*However, he would occasionally show such amazing tenderness and remorse that for two years I could never bring myself to leave him, despite the unhealthy influence he had on our daughter. Finally, at the urging of our marriage counselor, I escaped to my parents' home. With their love and support, I slowly began to pull away from the bonds of my attachment to David. But he, more and more urgently, tried to win me back. I feared him, yet at the same time I needed him; I felt unable to free myself from the relationship. All in all, I was overjoyed to think that my nightmare might finally be ended with his suicide.*

*I was heartbroken when he appeared again the next morning. He was very depressed and proceeded to tell me the events of the night before. He admitted he had been planning to kill himself. He had gotten pills from a friend and had waited until nighttime so that nobody would be able to find him. Then he had sat down to compose his suicide note and will. After he had typed a few lines, the power suddenly went out. There wasn't even enough light for him to finish his note by hand. Without that sense of completion, he had been unable to go through with his plans. Then he told me that perhaps fate had interfered to keep him alive and that this was a sign that he and I still belonged together.*

*As he told me this story, I felt fury. I had come so close to being free of him, finally so close, and one tiny twist of fate had ruined it for me. I was still stuck with this cruel, unstable man, the man who had destroyed my confidence, who showed every intention of tormenting me the rest of my life. I had never been so consumed with hate. My disappointment was so intense, I decided immediately what I would have to do. I knew, especially given his current emotional state, that if I handled the situation the right way he would likely try suicide again. So I opened my mouth to say, coldly, that I still thought he was a horrible monster and that I would never come back to him no matter what he did. I was about to say that I didn't care if he lived or died and that if anything, I preferred him dead. I was prepared to be as cruel as necessary to drive him back to suicide.*

*But then I paused. I still raged with hate, but I paused. I saw how close I was to encouraging a human being to die and was shocked by how far I was willing to carry my hate. I looked at him and was suddenly struck by something—something I learned at Camp Moriah. I was struck by his personhood, his humanity. Here before me was a person. A person with incredible emotional problems to be sure, but a person nonetheless. With his own deep hurts. His own heavy burdens. He himself had been raised in an abusive environment, with very little love and almost no kindness.*

*These thoughts made me cry. To my surprise, however, these were not tears of despair but tears of compassion. After all, this was a man who had intended to end his life.*

*I found myself putting my arm around him to comfort him. It's a moment I still can't fully comprehend. In spite of everything he had done to me, I was consumed with love. And most surprising to me of all, from that moment—the moment I began seeing David as a person—I was never again tempted to return to the relationship. I had thought loving David meant I had to stay. That's partly why I had felt trapped. But it turned out in my case that being freed from the need for justification for not loving him is what allowed me to leave—and to do so compassionately and calmly, without the bitterness that could have burdened me for a lifetime.*

*Just as I learned at Camp Moriah, when I started seeing people, the world transformed around me. I now feel free— not just from an unhealthy relationship but from feelings that might otherwise have poisoned me. My life certainly would have been easier had I never married David. But I will always be glad I did not encourage him to die.*

Yusuf looked up from the letter. Clearing his throat, he said, "If someone is abused, my heart breaks for that person; what a cruel burden to have to carry. If I know such a person and he or she rages inside, should I be surprised? Of course not. Under such circumstances, I think to myself, *Who wouldn't?*"

He slowly placed the letter back in the folder on the table. "In the face of that question, however, I find great hope in stories like the one I just read to you. For such stories show me that it is possible to find peace once more, even when much of my life has been a war zone.

"Although nothing I can do in the present can take away the mistreatment of the past, the way I see others in the present determines how I carry forward the memories of those mistreatments. When I see others as objects, I dwell on the injustices I have suffered in order to justify myself, keeping my mistreatments and suffering alive within me.

"When I see others as people, on the other hand, then I free myself from the need for justification. I therefore free myself from the need to focus unduly on the worst that has been done to me. I am free to leave the worst behind me and to see not only the bad but the mixed and good in others as well."

Yusuf clasped his hands together and looked around the room. "But none of that is possible if my heart is at war. A heart at war needs enemies to justify its warring. It needs enemies and mistreatment more than it wants peace."

"Yuck," Ria said under her breath.

"Exactly, Ria. Yuck," Yusuf said. "A high-ranking Israeli political leader once said to me, 'We and our enemies are perfect for each other. Each of us gives the other reason never to have to change.' Unfortunately, the same is true in our homes and workplaces. The outward wars around us start because of an inward war that goes unnoticed: someone starts seeing others as objects, and others use that as justification for doing the same. This is the germ, and germination, of war. When we're carrying this germ, we're just wars waiting to happen."

"So what can we do about it?" Carol asked.

"To begin with," Yusuf said, "we need to learn to look for the ways we're needing to be justified."

# 12 · GERMS OF WARFARE

"Justification has some telltale signs," Yusuf began. "I've already mentioned a few—how we begin horribilizing others, for example. In fact, that sign is a subset of a whole category of signs that you might think of as exaggerations. When our hearts are at war, we tend to exaggerate others' faults; that's what we call horribilizing. We also tend to exaggerate the differences between ourselves and those we are blaming. We see little in common with them, when the reality is that we are similar in many if not most respects."

Pettis looked thoughtful. "What you're saying makes sense to me, and I think this happens on a larger scale between groups of people. Some groups of people justify their mistreatment of other groups by exaggerating the differences between them. And the more noticeable the difference, the easier it is to exaggerate it. I think that's why differences like race and gender and religion and class have historically been at the heart of so many conflicts. The more observable the differences the more we can easily exaggerate them. And the more exaggerated the differences, the more we feel justified in our group's mistreatment of the other."

"My parents and Pettis's parents marched in the civil rights movement," Gwyn added. "And we both have ancestors who were enslaved. So racism is at the heart of who we are as Black Americans."

"What's striking to me," Pettis said, "is that today we talk about how these conflicts are all about race, but the racism that fuels these conflicts is a way to justify the mistreatment, not the other way around." Pettis seemed to be processing aloud. "Seeing one race as inferior is a way of justifying the mistreatment of one race by another. The mistreatment of one group by another comes *first*. And *then* differences in race or religion—or any other differences—are exaggerated to justify the mistreatment."

Yusuf nodded in agreement. "This exaggeration of differences is connected to the labeling we talked about this morning."

"Exactly!" Gwyn slapped her thighs. "We find even more justification in our conflicts once we've lumped another person into a larger group that we can label.

"Precisely," Yusuf said. "This means that we do not mistreat others because their humanity is hidden behind a stereotype, but we stereotype them—we lump them into stereotyped groups—in order to justify our mistreatment of them."

Ria, who had been listening attentively, spoke up: "I'm not sure that people experience this process so... sequentially. Most people, it seems to me, demean others because it's something they picked up in their families or their community. Their brains get stuffed with these stereotypes from the beginning."

"Exactly," Gwyn said. "I was thinking the same thing. Most people just accept what they're raised to believe about others, but it's not always that way. I can think of many people who reject the prejudices they were fed. There were White Americans who marched with our parents—they stood up for equality despite whatever ideas they were raised with."

"Yes," Yusuf agreed. "The humanity of others is always calling out to us. And despite the most strident prejudices and phobias that have been a part of a person's upbringing, the humanity of others is always calling. And as you've said, Gwyn, some people hear that call."

"This makes a lot of sense to me," Ria interjected, "but I want to make sure I understand what you're saying and what you're not saying. I hear you saying that we exaggerate the differences between us in order to stay blind to our shared humanity.

"But isn't it also true that if we really see others as people, that we could begin to appreciate the differences more than we ever had before? I mean, don't we sometimes assume that people are just like us, that there are no real differences, until we become curious enough and interested enough to get to know them at a deeper level?"

"Yes," Pettis said. "People often try to assure me that they aren't racist by saying that they don't see the color of my skin. But of course they see my skin color, and saying that they don't isn't just not true, but it makes me feel that they don't want to understand the things that make me who I am. To be Black in this country means something. If you don't see that, then you don't see me. The people that have seen me see my color because that's an important part of who I am, and they try to understand that and all the other things that make me who I am. I like your word, Ria. They are curious."

"I agree, Pettis," Yusuf said. "When we see others as people, we are endlessly curious about what makes others different and unique without exaggerating and using those differences to justify marginalization or mistreatment.

"These are important insights. In my experience, with Mordechai I had never become curious about him because I didn't see him as a person. And in order to feel justified for not helping him, I exaggerated the differences between us. But our tendency to exaggerate doesn't end there. When we betray ourselves, we will also tend to exaggerate the importance of anything that will justify us. If I had had an appointment around the time Mordechai spilled his coins, for example, it would have suddenly seemed critical that I get to it. If I had happened to be carrying a book with me, I might have suddenly felt the need to bury my nose in it and start reading. Whenever we need to be justified, anything that will give us justification will immediately take on exaggerated importance in our life. Self-betrayal corrupts everything—even the value we place on things."

Yusuf glanced at the board. "And consider, when in this experience with Mordechai did I start to devote my energy to blaming others? Before I betrayed myself or after?"

"After," Pettis said.

"And when in the story did I start feeling like a victim?"

"After you betrayed yourself," Ria said.

"And when in the story did I become consumed with the question of who's right and who's wrong? After I betrayed myself or before?"

"After," Ria said.

"Are you noticing a pattern?" Yusuf asked. "I betrayed myself, and my whole world changed. It changed because I had chosen a different way of being in the world—a way that needed justification. Because I needed justification, I began to see everything in a self-justifying way. Others, myself, the world, my past, my present, my future, my hardships, my responsibilities, my view of everything became transformed—transformed for the purpose of feeling justified.

"As we betray ourselves over time, we develop characteristic styles of self-justification. One person, for example, might find justification in seeing himself as being better than others. If I think I am superior, I can excuse a lot of sins. Another might find justification in feeling he is entitled to things he isn't getting. After all, if others aren't giving me what they should, it isn't my fault if I blame them or treat them poorly. And so on."

"There are countless ways to feel justified," Yusuf said, "but I would like to introduce four common styles of justification. These are justification styles that all of us carry to one degree or another, but we might find that some of them are bigger for us than others. My hope is that pointing out these styles will help us to see ourselves a little more clearly and to discover some ways in which our own hearts are warring."

Yusuf picked up a red marker. "The first of these is a style you'll immediately recognize in my experience with Mordechai. It's what we call the better-than style of justification, which is illustrated by the better-than box. This style of justification does not allow us to see others as people because we must see them prejudicially, as less than we are—less skilled, perhaps, or less important, less knowledgeable, less righteous, and so on, but always less and therefore always objects."

Yusuf drew the following:

## THE BETTER-THAN BOX

| VIEW OF MYSELF | VIEW OF OTHERS |
|---|---|
| Superior | Inferior |
| Important | Incapable/Irrelevant |
| Virtuous/Righteous | False/Wrong |
| **FEELINGS** | **VIEW OF WORLD** |
| Impatient | Competitive |
| Disdainful | Troubled |
| Indifferent | Needs me |

"I have a question." Pettis said.

Yusuf completed the quadrants of the box. "Sure, go ahead."

"What if someone really is less talented at something, for example, and if I really am better in that area? Are you suggesting it's a self-justification simply to note that?"

"Not necessarily," Yusuf said. "I can notice people's relative strengths and weaknesses when I'm seeing them as people. What's different when I'm in this box, however, is that I feel superior to or better than others because of these strengths or weaknesses. I use them to keep score of my and others' relative worth. So when I'm in this box, I'm doing more than simply noticing differences; I'm making judgments about people's worth based on those differences."

Pettis looked like he had another question brewing, but didn't speak up.

"Here," Yusuf said, "let me illustrate with a story. A few years ago, my wife, Lina, and I went out to a nice restaurant to celebrate Valentine's Day. When the hostess seated us, I immediately caught a whiff of the most foul body odor imaginable. I mean, I almost started dry heaving. And it was coming from the next table! As I looked in that direction, I noticed the rough-looking man who was obviously the source. I was furious. *How dare he come out in public this way! And on Valentine's Day of all days! He's going to ruin our evening!* In no time, this guy was an inconsiderate, filthy scumbag in my book."

"Well, you were quite the gentleman yourself," Elizabeth quipped.

"I was just noticing another's deficiencies," Yusuf said, keeping a straight face.

Elizabeth chuckled.

"Speaking of deficiencies," Yusuf said, "Lina didn't seem too bothered by the smell. I'm not sure what bothered me more—the smell or Lina not being bothered by it. I began badgering her and complaining so much that Lina finally asked the waiter to seat us elsewhere. Thankfully, from our new location in the next section of the restaurant, I could only faintly smell the guy's special perfume.

"When our food came, however, the stench came with it! *Did the waiter stink too?* He looked clean enough, so I looked around to see if the smelly man had just walked near us. But he was still seated across the way at his table. Then I noticed that the stench was coming from my plate of food! It turns out that this restaurant's black beans had a peculiar smell to them—a smell I had mistaken as body odor."

"Who would have thought—scumbag beans!" Elizabeth was enjoying herself.

"Right," Yusuf laughed.

"That's a nice story, turning out like it did," Gwyn said. "But what if the man really did stink? What if you weren't mistaken?"

"That's exactly the question I want to ask as well, Gwyn," Yusuf said. "What about that?" He looked around at the group. "What if I was right?"

"I have a thought about that," Elizabeth said, "as I've been in this kind of box ever since we began this morning."

"Really," Yusuf said. "How so?"

"I have been upset at my sister for not making the effort to be here for her boy. Someone had to come, so I came for her. That's a dangerous combination of facts for someone who is prone to feeling superior, isn't it?" Elizabeth blew the hair out of her eyes in mock exasperation. "I've been sitting here thinking about this while you've been talking, and here's what's occurred to me: I still think she should have made the sacrifice to come. I think I am right about that. But I haven't been able to stop at simply noticing the problem. I've been obsessing over it. I'm wallowing in unproductive thoughts and feelings as much as you, Yusuf, were wallowing in the stench."

Yusuf smiled. "So you're suggesting that even if I am right about something, my emotional experience will be entirely different in the box than it would be if I were out."

"Well, yes, something like that," she said. "Just like you've written there in the feelings area of the box, I've been impatient about being here, and I'm filled with disdain for my sister and her husband for not earning more, not making this the financial priority they should. I'm fixated on how they are a problem family, how my sister has always made poor choices in my eyes, how they fail their children, and so on."

Elizabeth's fluid speech slowed and stuttered. "I think I have made myself into an insufferable know-it-all."

"If that's true," Yusuf said, "you'll have that in common with a lot of us. I certainly justified myself in this way toward Mordechai, didn't I?"

Most seemed to agree, but Elizabeth was somewhere else.

"Let's consider a second common style of justification, shall we?" he said, as he walked to the board. "It's a style we call the I-deserve box.

"By the way," he added, as he began to write, "people who go around feeling better-than generally feel entitled to a lot of things, so these two styles of justification often come together."

## THE I-DESERVE BOX

| VIEW OF MYSELF | VIEW OF OTHERS |
|---|---|
| Meritorious | Mistaken |
| Mistreated/Victim | Mistreating |
| Unappreciated | Ungrateful |
| **FEELINGS** | **VIEW OF WORLD** |
| Entitled | Unfair |
| Deprived | Unjust |
| Resentful | Owes me |

Yusuf finished writing and turned to the group. "When I'm in this kind of box, I typically feel mistreated, victimized, entitled, deprived, resentful, and so on. Did I have any of these thoughts and feelings in the Mordechai story?"

"Yes," the group answered.

Yusuf seemed surprised by the volume of the response. "Right. So if I had been alive to how such thoughts and feelings are designed to give me justification, I might have been able to recognize that something was crooked in how I was being. I might have been able to find my way back to seeing Mordechai merely as he was, as a person.

"But I didn't recognize my crookedness, of course, and I went on viewing Mordechai more or less as an object for many years. And most of the other Mordechais I met as well," he added. "Which is to say that I was feeling justified in both the better-than and I-deserve ways in the Mordechai story, and probably in the black beans story too. When I'm seeing others crookedly, what I need in that moment is justification, and I'll find it any way I can get it—whether by seeing myself as better, as entitled, both, and so on."

It had been a while since Lou had said anything. When Yusuf looked over at him, he wasn't sure how to read the expression. Introspective or zoned out?

Yusuf got back to the story. "Before we leave behind the black beans, I want to address two additional points: First of all, notice how my better-than and I-deserve boxes set me up to be mistaken about this man. When would I be more likely to mistake the source of the offensive odor—when I look disdainfully and resentfully at others or when I simply see people?"

"When you look disdainfully and resentfully at them, no question," Pettis said.

"So notice," Yusuf said, "the more sure I am that I'm right, the more likely I will actually be mistaken. My need to be right makes it more likely that I will be wrong! Likewise, the more sure I am that I am mistreated, the more likely I am to miss ways that I am mistreating others myself. My need for justification obscures the truth."

Yusuf paused to embrace the quiet of the room. "One more point about the story before we move on. In order to make it, I'm going to change the scenario slightly. Let's say this story happened at home or in the workplace. Let's also assume, as Gwyn brought up earlier, that this person really did have a body odor problem. In that case, which version of me—the better-than, the I-deserve, or the seeing-person version—do you suppose would be more likely to be able to help him overcome his problem?"

"The seeing-person version. That I-deserve version isn't helping anything," Pettis said.

"Why?"

"Well, if you went to him when you were thinking he was a filthy lowlife or when you felt he owed you something, you'd probably just invite him to resist you."

"Does everyone agree with that?" Yusuf asked.

"I'm not sure that I do." It was Lou, fresh cup of coffee in hand, ready to engage. "I'm worried that if you just saw him as a person, you might not talk to him at all. You might just let it slide."

Yusuf almost looked pleased by the challenge. "You're still worried that seeing others as people means you have to be soft, aren't you, Lou?"

"Maybe I am, maybe I'm not." Lou sipped from the disposable cup. "It just seems like you might let this kind of thing slide rather than hurt someone's feelings. That's all I'm saying."

"Would I be likely to just let it slide if I really cared about the man?" Yusuf said. "Would I just let him stink and therefore let everyone think poorly of him? Is that what someone who really cares about another is likely to do?"

Lou leaned back, shaking his head.

"In fact," Yusuf said, "when I let people go on hurting themselves and others without making the effort to help them to change, it is rarely because I am seeing them as people. Usually it's because I am being motivated by yet another kind of self-justification, a justification that very often causes people to go soft and to feel justified by their softness."

"Now that is something I would be interested in hearing about," Lou said.

"I thought you might."

# 13 · MORE GERM WARFARE

Yusuf gestured toward Avi, who had been hanging back by the beverage table. "Avi will tell you that his most common justification style invites him to act soft."

The group looked over at Avi.

"True enough," Avi said as he moved toward the drawing board at the front of the room. "When we find justification in softness, it's usually because we're carrying around a third basic kind of justification box, a box we call the need-to-be-seen-as box."

He picked up a green marker. "It looks something like this."

## THE NEED-TO-BE-SEEN-AS BOX

| VIEW OF MYSELF | VIEW OF OTHERS |
|---|---|
| Need to be well thought of | Judgmental |
| | Threatening |
| Fake | My audience |
| **FEELINGS** | **VIEW OF WORLD** |
| Anxious/Afraid | Dangerous |
| Needy/Stressed | Watching |
| Overwhelmed | Judging me |

"When I'm carrying around this kind of box," Avi said, as he finished up the diagram, "I might be worried about being seen as likable, for example. Such a box will keep me from being able to do the helpful and right thing when the helpful or right thing might be something the other person won't like."

Carol leaned forward. She wanted to hear this.

"Let me give you an example," Avi said. "Early on in our time here at Camp Moriah, I hired a man named Jack as our field director—the person who runs everything out on the trail with the youth. It didn't take me too long to discover I had made a mistake. It turned out that Jack was a very poor manager of people. He had a bad temper and always blamed problems on others. He carried a better-than box that made out everyone he worked with to be inferior. As a result, he dismissed criticism out of hand, blamed every failure on others, and generally treated his coworkers with indifference and disdain. He was creating problems everywhere. I saw what was going on, of course, and knew that if he was ever going to make it here, he simply would have to change the way he worked and the way he managed. But you know what? I never said anything to him about it. He had a pretty volatile personality, and I was afraid to confront him with the problem. So I didn't. Instead, I just started hoping he would move or decide to take another job!"

"See, that's what I'm talking about!" Lou looked relieved. "That's exactly what has me worried about what you're saying here—that it will make people paralyzingly soft."

"But was I seeing Jack as a person in this story, Lou?"

Lou thought for a moment. He wanted to say yes, but it wasn't that simple.

"If he'd have been a person to me, then I would have cared enough about him to want to help him succeed, don't you think?" Avi said.

Lou didn't say anything. He saw that he was on the losing side of this one.

"I agree, Lou, that my softness here as a manager was a problem. But I would suggest that in this case I was soft precisely because I saw Jack as an object, not because I saw him as a person. I had a need-to-be-seen-as box about being likable, or perhaps about not having problems, which caused me to completely ignore what would have been most helpful to Jack and to Camp Moriah. As Yusuf mentioned a moment ago, this kind of justification box—the need-to-be-seen-as variety—often invites us to go soft."

Lou found himself nodding.

Yusuf jumped in. "This is also the kind of justification that Teri noticed in the Mordechai story, when she reasoned that my turning away might have been motivated by a desire not to appear callous. In other words, I was presenting an image of myself; I had a need for others to see me in a way that justified my inaction. This is the kind of justification box that was behind me pushing the lettuce under the counter, where no one could reasonably argue that I should have seen it and therefore have picked it up. My pushing the lettuce away shows that I had a need to be seen as considerate or responsible or tidy—qualities others would not ascribe to me if they thought I consciously left the lettuce there. Of course, the fact that I didn't just bend over and pick it up, which couldn't have taken any more energy than scooting it away, suggests that I might also have been carrying around one of the earlier justification boxes we discussed. Which one, would you say?"

"You're too important to pick up lettuce," Gwyn answered. "It sounds to me like you have a better-than box."

"Yes, Gwyn, excellent," Yusuf said. "I think that's right. Which means, put another way, that I saw Lina as just unimportant enough that she should be the one to have to worry about that kind of thing."

He played with the marker in his hand. "How would it be to live with someone who thought of you like that?"

Lou felt his chest tighten. He hadn't bent over to pick up the lettuce leaves or their equivalents in his home for years, if ever. He never bothered to hide the evidence either. It didn't matter to him that something fell on the floor; he couldn't be bothered by such trivialities. Yusuf's words rang in his head: *I saw Lina as just unimportant enough that she should be the one to have to worry about that kind of thing. How would it be to live with someone who thought of you like that?*

Lou wondered what Carol was thinking right now. A sensation crept up on him, one that was almost completely foreign and forgotten. It started as a prickly heat. He felt his ears go red and his cheeks flush. And then he knew—he was embarrassed!

He looked at the diagram of the better-than box—superior, important, virtuous, righteous, impatient, disdainful, indifferent; others are inferior, incapable, wrong, and so on.

He felt nailed.

On the plane Cory had said, "I suppose you think I've really done you wrong, Dad. You're even upset to be on this plane. You think it's just another waste of time I've caused you."

Cory was right. Lou had to admit it now. He resented being on that plane, having to spend this time away when his company was coming unglued. All because of a son who lacked even a shred of gratitude for everything Lou had offered him, a son who was ruining the family name.

The word "unfair" echoed in his brain. And there it was, looking back at him from the board: the I-deserve box—*you see life as unfair and others as ungrateful and mistreating. You are prone to resentment and to feelings of entitlement.*

It's true, Lou felt like he deserved more. A better son—like his older son, Jesse. Yusuf's words replayed: *How would it be to live with someone who thought of you like that?*

Lou shook his head as he scanned the diagrams. He paused at the need-to-be-seen-as box—need to be well thought of. *No, I couldn't give a damn,* Lou thought. *I don't have that one.* But then he noticed that this style of self-justification often sees others as threatening. *Ah, hell.* Instantly he knew that he did see Cory that way. Cory threatened the family reputation and name. He put Lou's reputation at risk. *I do care what others think of me. A lot.*

Avi interrupted Lou's thoughts. "Finally, there is a fourth common category of self-justification. It came up in our discussion about Mordechai when one of you mentioned that Yusuf might have become depressed by the thought that he was actually a bad person. This style is illustrated by the worse-than box." He drew the following:

## THE WORSE-THAN BOX

| VIEW OF MYSELF | VIEW OF OTHERS |
|---|---|
| Not as good | Advantaged |
| Broken/Deficient | Privileged |
| Fated | Blessed |
| **FEELINGS** | **VIEW OF WORLD** |
| Helpless | Hard/Difficult |
| Jealous/Bitter | Against me |
| Depressed | Ignoring me |

"Can I ask a question about this one?" Carol said.

"Of course, Carol."

"I've been wondering about this kind of view since Yusuf shared his story about Mordechai." She hesitated. "Well, frankly, I see a lot of myself in this one, but I don't see how I feel justified when I'm seeing things in this way. In fact, if anything, I feel just the opposite. For example, when I was in the middle of my eating disorder, I just felt worthless and no good. I didn't feel justified at all."

Avi nodded. "Let me share something with you."

Lou put an arm around the back of Carol's chair as Avi began. "I had a speech impediment until I was nearly twenty. I stuttered terribly. I can't tell you how embarrassing it was. I pulled away from others and looked for every excuse to be alone. Did I know I had a problem? Yes. And it was my problem, I knew that. But it affected my view of others. I looked at them longingly, not out of any kind of love or concern, but rather out of a kind of nagging jealousy. I was jealous that I couldn't be more like them, jealous of how easily speech came to them. I was always afraid I would encounter a block, that my eyelids would flutter pathetically while I tried to spit out the words. I imagined this scene many times, and I lived in perpetual fear of looking ridiculous.

"So did I feel justified?" he said. "It depends what you mean by that. I wasn't justifying my stuttering, since stuttering itself doesn't need justification. There is no crookedness toward others in merely having trouble with speech—or in any other disability, for that matter. Although I wasn't justifying my disability, I was justifying something else. In fact, I was *using my disability* to justify something else—something that was crooked, something that required justification. I used my disability as justification for separating myself from others. This—the separation from others as people—is what needed justifying; it was this act that was crooked. I turned from people at every opportunity, not allowing myself to be touched by their needs, and blamed my disability all the while. I told myself that I couldn't be expected to do this thing and that given my disability. My disability was my justification! It was my excuse for failing to engage with the world."

Carol leaned back into Lou's arm. "Okay, I think I get it then," she said. "So in my case, it may not be that I was feeling justified for my eating disorder but that I might have started to use my disorder as an excuse for why I couldn't be better with others."

"That is worth thinking about," Avi said. He looked back at the boxes he and Yusuf had written on the board. "As I look at these boxes and compare my early life against them, I would say that I can certainly relate to the worse-than box. I would say that I can relate as well to the need-to-be-seen-as box. In fact, in my life the need-to-be-seen-as and worse-than justifications have often come together. While suffering from my stuttering, I desperately wanted others to think well of me. As a result, I almost never spoke because I was afraid that I would look foolish. Just as that box suggests, I viewed others as judgmental and threatening, and I always felt as if I was being watched, listened to, and evaluated. Cutting myself off from others as people, I lived in constant fear and anxiety. And the more I cut myself off from them, the more the anxiety grew."

"Yes, I can see that in myself as well," Carol said. "I think I sometimes pull away and try to just slink off into the shadows. Lou here is such a successful and accomplished person, a lot of times I don't think that I measure up, and I end up getting really down on myself."

Lou squeezed Carol's knee.

"I know the feeling," Avi said. "I spent most of my first twenty years feeling the same way."

"What did you do about it?" Carol asked. "Was it just as simple as getting rid of your stutter?"

Avi smiled. "Believe me, getting rid of the stutter wasn't easy at all."

"No, that's not what I meant," Carol said, turning pink.

"I know, I know," he said. "I'm just teasing. But in answer to your question, Carol, stuttering wasn't the problem."

Avi looked down at the floor. "Nope. Stuttering wasn't the problem," he repeated. "The truth is, even after I'd mostly overcome my stuttering, I tried to commit suicide. Two attempts, actually."

This seemed to suck the air out of the room.

"One time with pills, one time with a razor blade." Avi dug his hands deeper into his pockets. "The second time around, my mother found me on the bathroom floor in a pool of blood."

# 14 • THE PATH TO WAR

"So no, Carol," Avi said, "my stuttering was not the cause of my problems. Rather, I carried a heart at war—a heart at war with others, myself, and the world. I had been using my stuttering as a weapon in that war and had gotten myself into a place where I was seeing crookedly and feeling self-justified. That was my problem. And I wasn't able to find my way out of it until I found my way out of my need for justification."

"How?" Carol asked.

Avi smiled at her. "That, Carol, will be our topic for tomorrow."

"You're going to leave it at that?" Lou sounded invested—or perhaps overcaffeinated. "You just told us you tried to commit suicide twice and now we're just going to leave for the evening?"

Avi chuckled. "You want to hear more about it?"

"Well, I don't know. Maybe."

"I'll tell you more about it tomorrow," Avi said. "But in our last forty minutes or so this evening, I think it would be best to review what we've covered today. That way, we'll come back tomorrow with a solid understanding."

Elizabeth looked okay with this decision. Jet lag was sinking in.

"First of all," Avi said, "we've talked about two ways of being: one with a heart at war, where we see others as objects, and the other with a heart at peace, where we see others as people. And you'll remember that we learned that we can do almost any behavior, whether hard, soft, or anything in between, in either of these ways. Here are two questions for you then: If we can do almost any outward behavior with our hearts either at peace or at war, why should we care which way we are being? Does it matter?"

"Yes," Carol said. "It definitely matters."

"Why?" Avi asked. "Why do you think it matters?"

"Because I've seen how a heart at war ruins everything."

Avi waited for more.

Carol sighed. "I've been acting outwardly nice toward our boy Cory ever since he started getting into trouble, but I've known that I didn't really mean it. And this has done a couple of things to me. First of all, I think I have played into an I-deserve box that has me thinking I am being nothing but sweet and kind, and he's just mistreating me and the rest of the family. And Cory can tell that's how I'm feeling. I know because he's called me on it many times."

She gave a sad laugh. "Of course, I always deny his accusations. I think I've spent most of the last few years feeling a gnawing guilt knowing that I'm not really loving Cory, even though I've been making it look like I do." Her eyes filled with tears. "And no good mother does that." She shook her head, wiping her eyes with a fist. "No good mother does that. I think I've developed a worse-than box—that I'm a bad mom."

"I think you're being too hard on yourself," Lou said. "The truth is Cory has been a terribly difficult boy. It's not your fault."

Carol tool a deep breath. "It depends what you mean. I understand that I may not be responsible for the things he's done. But I am responsible for what I've done."

"Yes, but you've done nothing but good," Lou offered. "I'm the one who's been the jerk with him."

"But Lou, don't you see? We're talking about something deeper than merely what I've done or haven't done. Yes, I've cooked his meals and cleaned his clothes. I've stood there and taken his abusive language, and more. But that's just on the surface. The point is that while I've been playing the part of the outward pacifist, my heart has been swinging at him. *And* at you for the way you outwardly war with him. I've been at war too, but just in a way that makes it seem like I'm not."

"But who wouldn't be, under the circumstances?" Lou said. "At war, that is."

"But that can't be the answer, Lou! It can't."

"Why not?"

"Because then we're all doomed. That's to say that our entire experience, even our thoughts and feelings, is controlled and caused by others. It's to believe that we're not responsible for who we've become." Carol wiped her eyes again and looked around the room, feeling both embarrassment and comfort at seeing the attentive faces.

"But damn it, Carol, don't you see what Cory is doing? He's making you feel guilty for stuff he's doing. What about Cory being responsible?"

Avi saw Carol's discomfort with the attention of the room. "It's a good question, Carol. What do you think?"

"I think…" Carol interlaced her fingers. "I think if we can't react to a heart that's at war with anything but warring hearts ourselves, how can we expect or demand that he act any differently to us?"

"But he caused it all!" Lou said. "We've always given him everything he's needed! It's his fault! You're about to let him off the hook and take it all upon yourself. I won't allow it!"

Carol felt the tears spring to her eyes again. She took a deep breath and exhaled slowly.

Yusuf spoke up. "What are you afraid of, Lou?"

"Afraid? I'm not afraid," Lou said.

"Then what is it you feel you cannot allow?"

"I can't allow my boy to get away with destroying my family."

Yusuf nodded. "You're right, Lou. You can't."

This answer confused Lou.

"But that is not what Carol is suggesting. She hasn't said anything about letting Cory off the hook. She's only been talking about not letting herself off the hook."

"No, she's sitting here blaming herself for things that are Cory's fault."

"Like what? Has she said that the drugs and the stealing were her fault?"

"No, but she's saying that she's been a bad mother, when the fact of the matter is that any halfway good son wouldn't have ever made her feel that way."

"And Cory didn't, that's her point," Yusuf said.

"Didn't what?"

"Didn't make her feel that way."

"Yes, he did!"

"That's not what I heard *her* say."

Lou turned to Carol. "Look, Carol." Carol's eyes were closed. "I know you're upset, but I don't want you to take on more than you are able or internalize problems that aren't yours, that's all."

Carol blinked back the tears and looked at Lou. "I know, Lou. Thank you. But Yusuf's right."

"Right about what?"

"That I am responsible for how I have been feeling, not only for what I have been doing."

"But you wouldn't have been feeling that way if it wasn't for Cory!"

"You may be right."

"See!" Lou said. "That's what I mean."

"Yes, but it's not what *I* mean."

Lou furrowed his eyebrows.

"The fact that I wouldn't have felt the way I've come to feel if it weren't for Cory doesn't mean he has caused me to feel as I have."

"No, that's exactly what it means," Lou said.

"No, Lou, it doesn't. And here's how I know: I'm not feeling that way now. Cory has done everything he has done—everything I've blamed him for, all the ways I've felt about it—but I don't feel the same now. Which means that he hasn't caused me to feel how I've felt. I've always had the choice."

"Choice!" Lou almost laughed. "He sure makes the choice difficult!"

"Yes," Yusuf stepped in. "He likely does, Lou. But difficult choices are still choices. No one, whatever their actions, can deprive us of the ability to choose our own way of being. Difficult people are nevertheless people, and it always remains in our power to see them that way."

"And then get eaten up by them," Lou said.

"That's not what he's saying, Lou!" Carol seemed surprised by her own voice. "Seeing someone as a person doesn't mean you have to be soft. The Saladin story showed us that. Even war is possible with a heart at peace. But you know that, Lou. You've been here the whole time I have, and you're a smart man. Which means that if these are really still questions for you, then you are refusing to hear. Why, Lou? Why are you refusing to hear?"

For the second time that day, Carol knocked Lou completely off balance. She had never criticized Lou so directly. Certainly never in front of others. And yet here she was, countering Lou's complaint that she was letting others off the hook by refusing to let Lou off the hook! Lou had two thoughts simultaneously: *This is idiotic,* and *This is miraculous: here I am learning lessons on outward toughness from a pacifist.* He had worried that this course would invite people to be weak and soft, but Carol seemed to be metamorphosing in the other direction right before his eyes. All this heart-at-peace stuff was making her more direct, not more soft.

"Lou," came Yusuf's voice. "Are you okay? We all need to take our own time with these concepts."

"Yes, fine. I'm fine."

He leaned over to Carol. "I think I may be recovering a bit of my hearing," he whispered. Carol's smile relaxed the tightness in his chest.

Yusuf clapped his hands together and looked around at the group. "In response to Avi's question, Carol has suggested that the issue deeper than our behavior—our way of being—matters. A lot. Do you agree?"

Lou gave a nod along with the others.

"Then I have another question for you. If the choice of way of being is important, then how do we change from one way to the other? Specifically, how do we change from peace to war—from seeing people to seeing objects?"

"Through self-betrayal," Elizabeth said.

"Which is what?" Yusuf asked.

"It's what you illustrated through your experience with Mordechai. You had a sense to help him, which means you were seeing him as a person, but then you turned away and began to justify why you shouldn't have to help him, and he became an object to you."

"Yes, excellent, Elizabeth," Yusuf said. "So self-betrayal—this act of violating my own sensibilities toward another person—causes me to see that person differently, and not only them but myself and the world also. When I ignore a sense to apologize to my son, for example, I might start telling myself that he's really the one who needs to apologize, or that he's a pain in the neck, or that if I apologize, he'll just take it as license to do what he wants. And so on."

Lou wondered if Yusuf was looking at him intentionally.

"Which is to say," Yusuf continued, "that when I violate the sensibility I have about others and how I should be toward them, I immediately begin to see the world in ways that justify my self-betrayal. In those moments, I am beginning to see and live crookedly, which creates the need within me to be justified."

"But what if I don't have those impressions to help to begin with?" Lou asked. "I actually don't think I have them very often, to tell you the truth. Does that mean I'm not betraying myself?"

"Perhaps." Yusuf shrugged. "Yet it could mean something else."

"What?"

"What do you suppose happens if I get in this box here toward Mordechai and then don't get out?" Yusuf asked pointing to the Choice Diagram.

# THE CHOICE DIAGRAM

## SENSE/DESIRE

**Help Mordechai by gathering his coins for him**

(I'm seeing Mordechai as a PERSON with needs,
cares, worries, and fears that matter, like mine do)

**My Heart Is at Peace**

↓

## CHOICE

↙  ↘

Honor the sense  Betray the sense

↓  ↓

I continue to see
Mordechai as a
person like myself

I begin to see
Mordechai in ways that
justify my self-betrayal;
he becomes an OBJECT
I blame

**My Heart Goes to War**

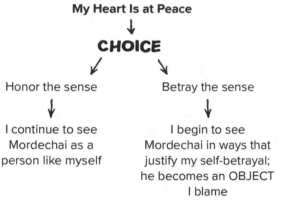

| VIEW OF MYSELF | VIEW OF MORDECHAI |
|---|---|
| Better than | Competitor |
| A victim (so owed) | No right to be there |
| Bad (but made to be) | Robs me of peace |
| Need to be seen as a | Zionist threat |
| good person | Bigot |
| **FEELINGS** | **VIEW OF WORLD** |
| Angry | Unfair |
| Depressed | Unjust |
| Bitter | Burdensome |
| Justified | Against me |

The group was quiet.

"Nothing will happen," Lou finally said. "Everything will stay the same."

"Yes, Lou, which is to say that I will end up carrying that box with me, right?"

"Yeah, I guess that's right." Lou spoke slowly, his mind trying to catch up to the implications.

"And if I carry this box with me," Yusuf continued, "then in my next interaction with Mordechai, I am likely to start in the box—from the very beginning, right?"

Yusuf scanned the room to check that everyone was following. "And if I'm already starting in the box, do you suppose it's likely that I'll have a sense or desire to help in my next interaction with Mordechai or with others I lump together with him?"

"No, you wouldn't." Lou leaned forward. "You would start out bothered and bitter and angry. And in that state you probably wouldn't have a sense to help at all."

"That's what I'm suggesting," Yusuf agreed. "I can end up living in a big box from which I already perceive people as objects. When I develop these bigger boxes, I erupt whenever my justifications in the box are challenged or threatened. If I need to be seen as smart, for example, I will get anxious whenever I think my intelligence might be at issue—as, for example, when I am asked to speak in public or when I believe others are evaluating me. If I feel superior, I will be likely to erupt in anger or disdain if others fail to recognize how I am better, or if I perceive that someone is trying to make himself look better than me. And so on. I no longer need to betray my sense regarding another in order to be in the box toward him because I am already in the box. I am always on the lookout for offense when I'm in the box, and I will erupt whenever my justification claims are threatened."

"So you're saying that if I don't have many senses toward others, it may be an indication that I'm already in a box, that I'm carrying my boxes with me, so to speak."

"I'm suggesting that possibility, yes."

Lou leaned back and crossed his arms.

"I have a different question from Lou's," said Carol.

"Sure, go ahead."

"My problem isn't that I have too few of these senses to help. I'm worried that I have too many. And frankly, as I think about this, I'm a bit overwhelmed that I have to do everything I feel I should do in order not to betray myself."

"I have the same question," Ria said.

Yusuf smiled. "It's a good thing, then, that that's not what this means."

"It's not?" Carol sounded relieved.

"No. And to see why not, let's look at the Choice Diagram again. Notice two elements of the diagram: First, notice that we use the words 'honor' and 'betray' rather than 'do' or 'not do.' Notice as well the word 'desire' along with 'sense.' In other words, this sense we're describing is something akin to a desire. You with me?"

Carol nodded. "Yes. 'Honor' and 'betray' and 'desire'—I see them."

"Okay, then, let me ask you this: have you ever been in a situation where you ultimately weren't able to do something you felt you should do for somebody but nevertheless still wished that you could have done it?"

"Sure, all the time," Carol said. "That's exactly what I'm talking about."

"Notice," Yusuf said, "how those experiences are different from this experience of mine. In my case, after I failed to help, did I still have a desire to help?"

Carol looked at the diagram. "No."

"No, I didn't. You're exactly right. So notice the difference: in my case, I started with a desire to help but ended with contempt, whereas in your case, you started with a desire to help and ended with a desire to help."

Carol looked down at her open notebook and scribbled something.

"Although it may be true in such cases that you didn't perform the outward service you felt would have been ideal, you still retained the sense or desire you had in the beginning. That is, you still *desired* to be helpful. My guess is that there were probably a number of other things that needed to happen, and you just couldn't do this additional ideal thing. Am I right?"

Carol nodded.

"And that's life." Yusuf shrugged. "We quite commonly have many things that would be ideal to do at any given moment. Whether or not we perform a particular service, the way we can know if we've betrayed ourselves is by whether we are still desiring to be helpful."

"Okay, I think I get it," Carol said. "So you're saying that the sense I'm either honoring or not is this desire of helpfulness, not the mere fact of doing or not doing any particular behavior."

"Yes, Carol, that's exactly what I'm saying. And that's why we use 'honor' and 'betray' on the Choice Diagram rather than 'do' or 'not do.'

"Incidentally," he continued, "this shows how I can actually behave the way I feel would be ideal but nevertheless still be in the box. Think about my experience with Mordechai again. Let's say that after I got in the box, I saw someone who knew me, and then out of shame, not wanting to appear insensitive, I turned and helped Mordechai gather his coins, all the while fuming that I was being made to do it. In that case, would I have been seeing him as a person while I was helping?"

"No."

"Had I retained my desire of helpfulness?"

"No, just the opposite."

"So had I honored or betrayed my sense of helpfulness?"

"You'd betrayed it," Carol said. "So it's not simply about the behavior, is it? It's deeper than that."

"Exactly. My heart wouldn't have been at peace, even though I was being outwardly helpful, which suggests a betrayal of my original desire to help."

Carol suddenly looked uncomfortable. "Then that raises another question for me."

"Go ahead."

"The situation you described—retaining my desire to help even when I can't help—explains some of my experiences but not all of them."

"Go on."

"Well, a lot of times, when I can't help, I don't think I feel peaceful anymore either. To be honest, sometimes I'm burning up inside. I feel overwhelmed—all anxious and stressed because I can't help. It eats me up, and I can't seem to relax or find peace. Like when my house isn't clean, for example. I get anxious when we have others over if I haven't been able to clean up."

"Ah," Yusuf said, "then in those cases it sounds like you might be in the box, doesn't it?"

Carol nodded.

"And you might, Carol. Ultimately, you're the only person who would know for sure, but it sounds like you might have developed a hyperactive need-to-be-seen-as box. Maybe you have a box about needing to be seen as helpful, for example, or thoughtful or kind or as a kind of superwoman. Any need-to-be-seen-as boxes like those would likely multiply in your mind the list of obligations you think you have to meet. And when you aren't able to meet them, they rob you of peace."

"That's me to a T." She almost laughed. "That's exactly what I'm like. But"—her face grew serious—"then where do they come from?"

"Where do *what* come from?"

"These boxes—like this need-to-be-seen-as box."

"Well, let's look at the Choice Diagram." Yusuf turned to face the board. "When in that story did I have a box—of the better-than, I-deserve, need-to-be-seen-as, or worse-than variety?"

"After you betrayed your sense."

"Exactly. Which is to say that we construct our boxes through a lifetime of choices. Every time we choose to pull away from and blame another, we necessarily feel justified in doing so, and we start to plaster together a box of self-justification, the walls getting thicker and thicker over time."

"But why have I developed a need-to-be-seen-as box as opposed to some of the others?"

"Good question, Carol," Yusuf said. "If you're like most people, you've probably developed boxes that have elements from each of these styles of justification."

"I think I'm usually in the worse-than or need-to-be-seen-as categories," Carol said.

"Not me," said Lou. "Better-than and I-deserve all the way."

"What a surprise," Gwyn joked.

"Yes, shocking," Elizabeth agreed.

"I wouldn't want to disappoint you," Lou said.

Carol guided them back. "So why do Lou and I have different kinds of boxes?"

"With respect to the box," Yusuf said, "don't be too taken in by the categories. They are simply linguistic tools that help us think a little more precisely about the issue of justification. The differences they show are in key ways artificial. What I mean is that our similarities are much greater than our differences. What you and Lou share with everyone else on the planet is a need to be justified that has arisen through a lifetime of self-betrayals. If we justify ourselves in different ways, it is because we justify ourselves within a context, and we will reach for the easiest justification we can find. So, for example, if I had been raised in a critical or demanding environment, it might have been easier for me, relatively speaking, to find refuge in worse-than or need-to-be-seen-as justifications.

Those who were raised in affluent or sanctimonious environments, on the other hand, may naturally gravitate to better-than and I-deserve justifications, and so on. Need-to-be-seen-as boxes might easily arise in such circumstances as well."

Carol listened intently.

"But the key point, and the point that is the same for all of us, is that we all grab for justification, however we can get it. Because grabbing for justification is something we do, we can undo it. Whether we find justification in how we are worse or in how we are better, we can each find our way to a place where we have no need for justification at all. We can find our way to peace—deep, lasting, authentic peace—even when war is breaking out around us."

"But how?" Carol asked.

"As Avi said earlier, that is our topic for tomorrow. For tonight, we invite you to ponder what boxes you are carrying and the nature of your predominant self-justifications."

Avi spoke up from the back of the room. "We also invite you to consider how your box—this warring heart that you carry within—has invited outward war between you and those in your life."

He moved toward the board and pointed at the picture of his conflict with Hannah about the edging. "Remember this Collusion Diagram? Look for that pattern in your own lives tonight," he said. "See where you might be inviting in others the very behavior you are complaining about. Ponder what boxes might be behind your reactions in those situations. Try to figure out what self-justifications you are defending."

Yusuf looked around at the group. "In short, our invitation to you for tonight is to notice your battles and to ponder your wars.

Using the conflict in the Middle East metaphorically, we are, all of us, Palestinian and Israeli in some areas of our lives. It will serve neither ourselves nor our loved ones to think that we are better.

"Have a good evening."

# PART III

## FROM WAR TO PEACE

# 15 • APOLOGIES

Lou barely slept that night. He tossed and turned as the mistakes of the last thirty years played themselves over and over in his mind. Cory was an object to him; he couldn't deny it. His heart stirred in anger just at the thought of Cory's name. But now there was a new feeling—a desire to be rid of the ache he felt regarding Cory rather than a desire to be rid of Cory. He wanted his son back. Or maybe more accurately, he wanted to be Cory's father again.

The ache didn't stop there. He felt the pain of pushing out Kate. That meeting in the boardroom replayed in the dark, his angry words echoing back at him. He'd acted like a child! He couldn't afford to lose Kate. Yet his pride had blinded him to a truth he suspected was obvious to everyone else—that Kate, not Lou, was the prime mover behind Zagrum's success.

In the early hours of the morning, his thoughts and pain were located elsewhere. He looked at Carol, soundly asleep next to him. For thirty-one years, she had given her life to him, while he had given too little in return. Lou felt the weight of their history together like a presence in the room.

They met at a dance at Syracuse University. Carol was on a date with one of Lou's friends. Lou, solo that night, couldn't take his eyes off her. He began the evening wondering whether it would be ethical to move in on his friend. By the end of the evening, it was no longer a matter of ethics, only of strategy.

Over the months that followed, Lou came to see Carol as a contradiction. On the one hand, she had a warmth and easy air about her—quick to laugh, always ready with an engaging or witty response. In a word, she was fun. Fun to talk to, fun to joke with, fun to be around. On the other hand, she was instinctively cautious. The obedient daughter of a preacher, she was raised to be wary of men and their intentions. Her father was fond of asking all of her suitors down to the basement to "see his trains." Once there, he threatened them with violence if they were to do anything improper with his daughter. He removed an old shotgun from the back wall to help illustrate his point. But the basement charade didn't scare Lou off; he had completely fallen for Carol Jamison. Now he knew that Mr. Jamison had to approve of him before Carol could fully fall in love with him.

He spent a lot of time with her father and his "trains."

Between dates with Carol and lectures from her dad, Lou's grade point average took a beating. But there was no turning back. He thought of Carol during class and study time anyway, so it was no good trying to rescue his grades by pulling away. Ultimately, Lou, who had not been raised in a religious home, won the trust of Carol's religiously devoted father, and he proposed. It was then that Lou learned a lesson about Carol's independence. She might have shared her father's caution, but she did not blindly act upon his approvals. When Lou first proposed, she told him she would have to think about it. He held onto the ring for five months before she finally allowed him to slip it on her finger. The moment would stay with Lou forever: they were driving home from a church service one rainy afternoon. Her words came out of the blue. "Yes, Lou, I will marry you."

The car swerved. "Excuse me?"

"I'll marry you, Lou. I'll devote my life to you and to our family."
And she did.

As Lou remembered this, he knew he had not returned the single-minded devotion. His eye never wandered to other women. That was not his vice. No, his problem was a constant obsession with himself—an obsession with his own success, his own station in the world.

It had started with seeming selflessness: his decision to enlist in the Marines and go to Vietnam. He began toying with the idea while Carol was mulling his marriage proposal. Perhaps out of fear of rejection, or maybe as a way to avoid public embarrassment if she were to finally reject him, or still yet out of a fervent patriotism, Lou had enlisted two days before Carol surprised him with her acceptance. It would be five years before they would walk down the aisle.

That was twenty-five years ago. Their first child, Mary, was born less than a year after that, and their second, Jesse, followed two years later. Lou's first company was "born" shortly thereafter, and with it a workplace obsession that left Carol to play the part of a single parent—emotionally, in any case, if not physically as well. Cory, their third child, was more than a day old before Lou made it to the hospital to see him and Carol. "The meetings in New York just couldn't wait," he had told her. They never could. They both knew, though, that Yale Hospital in New Haven was only a ninety-minute excursion from Wall Street.

Carol was hurt by his absence, but at that point she'd grown used to it. Lou didn't take well to being told what to do or when to do it, so she had learned over the years not to ask much of him.

The contradictory combination of her fierce devotion and steely independence is what held the family, such as it was, together. As he replayed the ritual phone calls from Carol asking if he would be home for one of the kids' evening events, he could see unfolding in front of him one moving image of Carol after another—in an auditorium, in a gym, on a soccer field, at a recital and a birthday party—snapping photos and cheering on the children. But always she was alone. And though he could see her in his mind's eye, he couldn't see the kids. He hadn't been there.

And Cory. Nothing had meant more to Cory than his leading role in *The Music Man* in the abbreviated production put on by his fifth-grade class. He practiced for weeks, singing incessantly throughout the house. And the production had played only one night. Lou's business meeting—was it in Tokyo?—had felt so important at the time. Now he couldn't even recall where it was, what it was about, or who was there. But he could see Cory's face clearly as he replayed the moment when he came home. "How did it go, buddy?" he had asked after dropping his suitcase in the foyer.

"It was okay." This was all Cory offered.

"Just okay? Tell me all about it!"

"It was fun. I really missed you, Dad." And then Lou had looked up to see Carol standing in the kitchen doorway, a dish towel in her hands, her face a mixture of frustration and pain. Lou had resented that face—and the disappointment that it seemed Carol was trying to put on. The resentment lingered and grew with each missed event. Couldn't she appreciate what he was doing? Couldn't they all appreciate what he was doing to provide so well?

But the resentment he had felt for so long was now gone. Her disappointment and pain was not put on. It was real. He could see it more clearly now than he saw it at the time. It was himself he was disappointed in all along.

In a very real way he had left her a long time ago. And coming to terms with what all these years must have been like for her was almost suffocating.

Lou checked the bedside clock again: 5:53 a.m. Any chance of sleep had come and gone. A crack of soft light ran down the window curtains. He sighed heavily as he got to his feet and headed for the shower.

Lou and Carol drove in silence to Camp Moriah. As they neared the offices, the pressure of his thoughts cracked him open. "Carol, I'm so sorry," he said. "Deeply sorry."

"For what?"

"For everything." He shook his head. "For not loving you as you have deserved to be loved. For not being there for you as you have always been there for me."

Carol didn't say anything for a moment. Her eyes started to water. "You've been there, Lou," she said. "Sometimes you've been other places as well, that's true. But you've always come home to me. Many women are not so fortunate. Not many can say that they've never had to worry, but I've never had to worry about you, Lou. Whatever else you might be devoted to, I've always known that you were devoted to me too."

"But it shouldn't have been a 'me too,'" Lou said. "That isn't good enough." Lou parked on the far side of the lot, away from the other cars. "I'm going to make it up to you. I promise."

After a moment's silence, Carol said, "You're not the only one who needs to apologize."

"What do you mean?"

"You know what I mean," she said. "I've been there for you, I suppose, but my heart hasn't necessarily been there. I've been blaming silently for years."

"But you've had every right to!" Lou meant it.

"Have I?" She turned to him. "The more I've become consumed with how my own needs aren't being met, the larger those needs have become, until I think I have numbed myself to the needs of others—to your needs, to Cory's."

"There you go beating yourself up again, Carol."

"No, Lou, beating myself up is what I've quietly been doing for years now. I'm not beating myself up now, I'm just finally noticing the internal fight."

"But all you've done for years is meet everyone else's needs, Carol. You've never lived for yourself at all."

"That's what I've been telling myself too, Lou, but it hasn't been true. I see that now." Carol looked straight ahead. "I've been hating you, Lou."

"Hating me?" Lou said this more to himself than Carol.

"Blaming you, in all kinds of subtle ways." She sighed. "Have I dutifully performed the household work? Yes. But that's just a behavior. Every time I've cleaned the house, I think I've buried myself a level deeper in self-pity. And I have spent years now feeling guilty for not feeling about you the way I know I should. It's been a downward spiral."

"It's me, Carol. Even with the bulimia, it was me. I've never seen it until now. I've spent so much time believing I deserved things and trying to control everything, including you. Gwyn helped me see this yesterday. She could see it, and I really didn't like her for that."

"And other things," Carol said, finally smiling.

"Look at my life, Carol! You and Kate and Cory. I alienate everybody. John too. I know I'm controlling. I get that. But I never thought I was sexist or racist. Gwyn is right. Look at my team. We're all White and Kate's the only woman I've ever had on the team. And now she's leaving because of me. I don't know, Carol. Everything's a mess."

Carol didn't know what to say. "So what are you going to do?" she finally asked.

"I don't know. I guess I hope to get more help today."

They sat in silence and watched as the other parents entered the building. Lou rubbed his forehead, a wave of tiredness hitting him. Carol wiped her eyes and checked herself in the rearview mirror. Time to join the others. Time to go deeper.

## 16 · A GIFT IN WARTIME

As they walked across the parking lot, Lou noticed Gwyn and Pettis pull into a parking stall. "Need to take care of something," Lou said to Carol. "I'll be in in just a minute."

"Gwyn, Pettis, do you have a second?" Lou called out.

"Sure," Pettis answered, though neither he nor Gwyn felt at all sure about Lou.

"Before we go in, I owe you both an apology. Mostly you, Gwyn. I was annoyed with you all day yesterday. You called me out more than once, and there aren't a lot of people in my life who are willing to do that. Not like you did."

"You're welcome?" Gwyn responded with what sounded like a question, completely caught off guard.

"I can see that I've created a life where people around me don't feel free to challenge me, Carol included. Anyway, I learned a lot from what you said yesterday, even though it was painful to hear. So thank you. And I'm sorry. You were right about a lot of things. I'm sorry."

"Please," Gwyn said, "we're all in the same boat here. But thank you. I really appreciate that. I think we're all discovering some things, no one more than me."

"Well, back into the furnace!" Pettis said with a laugh as he opened the door for the three of them.

"How was everyone's evening?" Avi gave a big smile as the group settled in their seats.

Lou looked around and was surprised to discover that he felt at home in the room, as if among friends. *Elizabeth, the proper Brit with subtle humor and surprising self-honesty. Ria and Miguel, the couple with an ongoing battle over the dishes. Jenny's quiet and timid parents, Carl and Teri. Pettis and Gwyn.*

"Lou, what's so funny?" Avi asked.

"Oh, nothing. It's just good to see everyone this morning, that's all."

In the comfort of the moment it was easy to forget how much had changed since the morning before.

"So, how do we get out of the box?" Avi twisted the marker in his hands. "How can our hearts turn from war to peace? That is the question for today."

"Good, because I sure want the answer," Lou said.

"Actually, Lou, you have already lived the answer," Avi said.

Lou smirked. "No, I don't think so."

"Sure you have. Just compare how you are seeing and feeling about everyone here today to how you were seeing and feeling about them yesterday morning."

It was as if someone suddenly turned on a bank of lights that Lou had grown accustomed to seeing without. His thoughts and feelings about this room and the people in it had changed. He could see it.

"Well, you're right. Things seem different to me this morning." He looked at Carol next to him, then back at Avi.

Avi smiled. "Grab a coffee, everyone. I'm going in for another story."

Lou raised his cup as a salute.

"Do you remember my stuttering and my suicide attempts?"

Everybody nodded.

"I'd like to tell you what happened. To do that, I need to go back to 1973."

Avi started pacing across the front of the room. "I celebrated my fifteenth birthday on October 5, 1973. The next day was Yom Kippur, or the Day of Atonement, the holiest day on the Hebrew calendar. It's a day of prayer and fasting in Israel, a day when everyone—even Israel's defense forces—gathers at home or in their synagogues in religious observance.

"Egypt and Syria launched a surprise attack that day at precisely 2:00 p.m.—Egypt from the south and Syria from the north. I'll never forget the piercing shriek of sirens that called the reservists from their worship and into uniform. My father, himself a reservist, raced from our Tel Aviv home within minutes. His unit was mobilized to the north, to fight back the Syrians along the Golan Heights.

"That was the last time I ever saw him."

Avi took a deep breath. "As a young boy raised on the David-and-Goliath-like tales of the Six-Day War, I expected him home within the week. But he was killed in a mortar attack three days later—one of many casualties in a place aptly called the Valley of Tears.

"My best friend was an Israeli Arab named Hamish. His father and mine worked at the same company. We met at an event the company threw for employee families. He lived in Jaffa, not too far from my home on the south side of Tel Aviv. We spent time together as often as we could.

"Of all the children I associated with in my youth, Hamish was the only one who never made fun of my stutter. It wasn't just that he never made outward fun of me, it was that I knew he never thought ill of me inwardly either. He was a true friend.

"When Hamish heard about my father, he came to grieve with me. But I was angry. I sent him away. I'll never forget the scene: Hamish, his head bowed reverently at my door while I forced out a string of butchered obscenities and blamed him for my father's death. I blamed him, my best friend, my only true friend. I told Hamish that he killed my father—him and everyone else who prayed and looked like him.

"I remember my whole body shaking with rage. Hamish didn't try to defend himself. In fact, he didn't say anything. He quietly left, and I watched him walk down the street and out of my life."

Avi looked down at the floor for a moment. "Two of the most important people in my life were suddenly gone—one a Jew, taken out by an Arab's weapon, and another an Arab, banished by the verbal bullets of a Jew.

"There was another casualty, of course. As we've learned, such a turn from the humanity of another requires extensive justification. In my mind, I began to exterminate a whole portion of the human race. Arabs were bloodsuckers, cowards, thieves, murderers—mere dogs who rightfully deserved death and were allowed to live only by the good graces of the Israeli people. What I didn't realize until years later is that whenever I dehumanize another, I necessarily dehumanize all that is human—including myself. What began as a hate for Arabs developed into a hate for any Jews who refused to share my hate for Arabs and nearly ended with a level of self-loathing that left me in a pool of blood on a bathroom floor in Tempe, Arizona.

"But that's how I met Yusuf." Avi looked to the back of the room where Yusuf stood, a cup of tea in hand.

"My mother, frightened by my depression after my father's death, had sent me to the United States to live with her brother. This was 1974. It was here that I learned to hate two other groups: first, the religious Jews, represented by my observant uncle, who insisted on looking to God when it was obvious that God—if there was one—was looking the other way; and second, the affluent Americans with all their toys and commercial gadgets, who looked suspiciously at the stuttering teenager who was forced to wear a *kippah*."

Avi placed his palm on his head, miming a skullcap.

"I wrestled with my stuttering as an act of survival and self-defense. By the time I enrolled at Arizona State University, I'd finally gained a kind of conscious control over it. But I was alone—cut off from the humanity that surrounded me. I was a solitary human soul.

"You might think that the isolation would have paid off in good grades." Avi chuckled, breaking some of the tension of his story. "Like many who are lonely, I was intensely preoccupied with others. Truth is, I was never really alone, even when I had physically separated myself, because I was thinking about my father, my people, the Arabs, and Hamish. Everyone I hated was always with me, even when I was alone. I needed them to be; I needed to remember what and why I hated in order to stay away from them.

"After a second suicide attempt and brief stay in the hospital, it was time to figure out my next move. The future seemed bleak. I had been placed on probation after my first year at ASU, and my second-year grades were even worse. I expected to be expelled. One day in early May, I received a letter from the provost's office— my expulsion notice.

"Or so I thought. In reality, it was a final, merciful lifeline. I was being invited to enroll in a forty-day survival program being run by one of the university's faculty—an Arab by the name of Yusuf al-Falah." He extended his arm toward Yusuf, who nodded.

"Which of course meant that I wasn't going to do it," Avi said. "I would rather be expelled than spend forty days and nights with a hatemonger, which is what I, as a hatemonger myself, assumed he must be. And I told my mother as much, who by then had moved to the States herself.

"'You will enroll in this program, Avi,' she told me. 'You've already tried to remove yourself from my life—twice—and the boy I once knew has been dead for years. You will not turn away from this opportunity, Avi. And why would you? Because of some blind grudge against someone you've never met?'

"As headstrong as I was, nobody defies my mother." The group laughed and the heavy air of the room lifted.

"And so I went," he said. "I went to live with my enemy."

The group waited for him to continue.

"So what happened?" Gwyn asked.

"Mind if I jump in?" Yusuf looked at Avi.

"Not at all," Avi said. "Please."

Yusuf walked to the front of the room. "To give you a feeling for what happened, perhaps it would help to tell you about something that happened here yesterday—with Carl and Teri's daughter, Jenny."

*Jenny!* Lou thought to himself. He couldn't believe he'd let her slip from his mind.

"I spoke to Teri and Carl this morning," Yusuf said, "and they said it would be all right for me to share this story with all of you. In fact, they haven't heard all the details yet, and I think it says a lot about the support of this group that they're comfortable opening it up to the room."

Teri and Carl nodded.

"When Jenny climbed in her parents' car yesterday morning, she was more than a little upset about the prospect of spending six weeks in a treatment program. You of course saw the state Jenny was in when she arrived and bolted across the street. You may not have noticed that she was without shoes. That may not seem vital at 9:00 a.m. But it's a different story when the Arizona sun begins to heat the city pavement, I can assure you. Even in April.

"As I mentioned yesterday afternoon, Jenny ran shortly after we began our session, and two of our young people set off after her. Here's what happened in the hours that followed."

"Hours?" Lou asked.

"Yes. The young people who followed her are named Mei Li and Mike. They were both students in our program and now work with us. Mei Li is twenty, and Mike, twenty-two.

"In fact, they are with us this morning," he said, extending his hand toward the back of the room.

The group whirled their heads around.

Mei Li and Mike, each of them comfortable in worn khakis and T-shirts, smiled back at them. Mike slipped the bandana from his head and tipped it, like ball players tip their caps. Mei Li waved sheepishly.

"Would you mind coming up and sharing what happened yesterday?" Yusuf asked.

They nodded and walked to the front.

"Well," Mike began, "Jenny took off running about fifteen minutes after you came into the building. She had a few blocks' head start when Mei Li and I took off after her. We called to Jenny as we caught up, but she yelled at us and started screaming about how her parents had betrayed her."

Mike paused. "No offense," he said to Carl and Teri.

Carl shook his head and waved the apology away. "Don't worry about it."

"Jenny was crying," Mei Li chimed in. "Nothing we said helped—maybe made it worse even. She started running faster and jumping walls trying to ditch us."

"She runs steeplechase," her mother said.

"Figures," Mei Li laughed. "We did our best to keep up."

"And we tried to keep up a conversation," Mike added. "That went on for a while—jogging after her and trying to talk. But then Mei Li noticed something."

"What happened?" Teri asked.

"Jenny's feet were bleeding. So we asked if it would be okay if we called someone to bring some shoes."

"Then what?" Teri said.

Mike shook his head. "She wouldn't have any of it."

Teri sighed.

"But then Mei Li sat down," Mike said, "and began removing her own shoes. 'Take mine then, Jenny,' she said. 'Your feet are beat up; mine are fine. Please.' But Jenny called her something I'd rather not repeat and kept running."

Jenny's father shook his head.

"Didn't matter though," Mike said. "Mei Li took off her shoes anyway."

"Mike did the same," Mei Li added. "He sat down and took his shoes off too. Then we tried to catch up to her."

"Barefoot?" Lou asked.

"Yeah," Mei Li said.

"For how long?" Lou asked.

"Oh," Mei Li said, "another three hours or so."

*"Three hours!"* Lou said. "Barefoot on the pavement? In Phoenix?"

"Yes." Mei Li seemed to be proud of this.

"But *why?*" Lou looked confused.

"That is the question," Yusuf said. "And I bet at the time, Mei Li and Mike couldn't have even articulated the reason. They just knew it was the thing to do."

"But it doesn't make any sense," Lou said. "She didn't want their shoes. All they did was beat themselves up."

Yusuf had grown accustomed to Lou's pushback. He smiled thoughtfully. "Actually, Lou, it makes the deepest sense in the world. And while they certainly inconvenienced themselves, their act accomplished something of great importance."

"What? What did it accomplish?"

# 17 · MARCHING BOOTLESS

"No, seriously, what good did that do—taking off their shoes?" Lou crossed his arms.

"It isn't so much what good it did," Yusuf said, "as what good it invited."

"Okay, then, what good did it invite?"

Yusuf looked at Mei Li and Mike. "Do you want to speak to that?"

"Sure," Mei Li said. She looked at Lou. "I'm not sure what good it invited, Mr. Herbert, but I know what happened—to Jenny."

*How does she know who I am?* Lou wondered.

"She decided on her own to enroll in the program. And I bet you wouldn't have predicted that."

"No," Lou agreed, "I can't say that I would have. How'd that happen?"

"Well, after a few hours, we finally ended up at some random mall. And Jenny ran into one of her friends. She started complaining about what her parents had done to her and about this program—how crazy it was. Of course, we're right there next to her, lurkin." Mei Li laughed. "So at some point she explains that we worked for that program and that we'd been following her all day.

"That's when her friend noticed Jenny's feet and our feet—all cracked and bloody—and asked that same question." Mei Li looked at Lou again. "She said, 'Barefoot? You've been running around the city barefoot?'"

Mike chimed in. "Yeah, Jenny kind of laughed at that. I think the absurdity of the situation was hitting her. And then her friend was laughing—and then we were all laughing, getting out all this tension."

"And then," Mei Li continued, "her friend looked at us and back at Jenny and said, 'Hell, Jenny, I'd never run around this city barefoot for you.' We were all cracking up. And then her friend was like, 'But seriously, Jenny. Maybe this thing will be a nice break for you. Figure some stuff out.'

"We talked for a while together after that, until her friend had to go. And after she left, Jenny turned to us and said, 'Okay then, tell me more about this Camp Moriah.'"

"So we answered everything she wanted to know," Mike said. "We told her about Yusi and Avi, about the wilderness we go to, and how we live off the land and how fun and interesting it is—how liberating."

"I don't know if she bought the liberating part," Mei Li laughed. "But she kept listening. And after talking for a while, you know what she said?"

The group hung on the answer.

"She said, 'Okay. I'll go.' She wasn't thrilled, no way. More resigned than anything, I think. But she was willing. And then during our ride back here together, just before we pulled into the parking lot, she said, 'I'm sorry for all the things I said to you today. And for your feet.' She was genuinely sorry. I know, because she was crying."

Jenny's mother looked like she was about to do the same.

"So, did taking our shoes off have anything to do with Jenny being willing to go out on the trail? I don't know for sure. You'd have to ask Jenny. But I do know what taking my shoes off meant for me. It was a way of joining Jenny in her world, which is something we always try to do here. It's a way to create space for helping people to get out of the box. So, for example, when we go out on the trail and the youth have nothing but a food pack and a poncho, we do the same. We have nothing more or less."

"Unless," Mike jumped in, "for safety reasons we have to have something else—a radio, for example, or a first-aid kit."

"Right," Mei Li said. "There are those differences. But we keep them to a minimum. Because if the kids had nothing but cornmeal to eat, for example, but I pulled out a candy bar for myself, how would that be treating them? Or if they had to sleep on the hard ground while I had an inflatable mattress, how would that be treating them?"

"As objects," came Miguel's gravelly voice.

"Exactly," Mei Li said. "I would be seeing myself as better than and more deserving than them. So how do you think that would invite them to see and treat me?"

"Same way," Miguel answered.

Mike nodded. "Getting on their level helps us invite their hearts to be at peace rather than go to war."

Mei Li looked at Lou. "So did it make a difference to Jenny? I don't know. But it made a difference to me. It helped me keep a heart at peace. And I think that might have made a difference to her. Like Yusi and Avi always tell us, we can't be agents of peace until our own hearts are at peace."

Lou sat stunned. Here was a twenty-year-old girl, probably less than two years removed from high school—and herself a delinquent in years past—who seemed to have a command of life that still seemed to escape him.

"Thank you, Mei Li and Mike," Yusuf said.

Many in the room echoed "thank you" as the two made their exit.

Turning back to the group, Yusuf added, "Do you think your children are in good hands now?"

Teri wiped her tears with a tissue and blew her nose. The others nodded.

"Well, then," Yusuf said. "You've now met our secret weapon— the young people here at Camp Moriah who work miracles in your children's lives. I'd like to discuss something that follows from what they just taught us.

"Most wars between individuals are of the *cold* rather than the *hot* variety: lingering resentment, old grudges, resources withheld, help not offered. These are the acts of war that most threaten our homes and workplaces. And the principles Mei Li shared with us apply no less in those environments than they do here on the trail with your youth. Think about our workplaces, for example. Think of the privileges we may retain for ourselves while we apply other standards to those who work with us or for us—privileges regarding vacation time, for example, or the choice parking spot, the special perks, the public spotlight, the differences between what we have to do to get something to happen and what everyone else in our organization has to do. Which of these are necessary or unavoidable, and which of them do we retain because we think we are better than others, more vital, and deserve special treatment?"

Lou couldn't help himself. "But what if you are?"

"More vital, you mean?"

"Yes."

"Then I would start wondering what special accommodations are vital in order for me to perform my vital function and what perks are simply personal indulgences. In other words, which of them are the candy bars and inflatable mattresses and which of them are the radios and first-aid kits?"

"But why should that be the question?" Lou asked matter-of-factly. "If I've worked all my life to get to where I am, shouldn't I be able to enjoy it?"

Yusuf smiled, enjoying the exchange. "Yes, Lou. Absolutely. And that's just the point, isn't it? Because everyone else wants to enjoy the fruits of their labors as well. The question for you as the leader is whether you are going to create an environment that is as enjoyable for your employees as it is for you—a place that they are as excited about and devoted to as you are. The best leaders are the ones people want to follow. We have a different word for people others follow only because of force or need. We call them tyrants."

*Tyrants.* The word triggered a memory for Lou. It was what one of his fired executives, Jack Taylor, had called him. No doubt what Cory would say as well.

Lou fell into his thoughts. Everyone who pulled up at Zagrum Company would know immediately which car was his, which office was his, which desk was his, which furnishings were his. He played by a different set of rules from the rest. Others had to get his approval for any expenditure over $2,000. He, on the other hand, could spend whatever he wanted whenever he wanted. He suddenly felt defensive. *But I'm the boss!*

"So what are you saying?" Lou said. "That I don't deserve anything extra for all that I've done? I built the company. It wasn't easy."

"Alone?" Yusuf asked.

"What?"

"You've built the company alone?"

"No, that's not what I meant."

"No? It's what you said."

"Well, it's not what I meant." Lou struggled to find the right words. "I mean that I led the company. It wouldn't have happened without me."

"I don't doubt it, Lou. No doubt at all. So here's the question: what's more important to you now—flaunting your well-earned important status or building a team and organization that will outlive you, surpass you, grow beyond you, and ultimately thank and honor you? What do you want, Lou?"

This question brought Lou squarely back to the mutiny in the boardroom. His executive team was fed up and gone. Now he really was alone, and the company was sinking. *No one would thank me, much less honor me. That kind of devotion was reserved for Kate.*

*Kate.* Just thinking her name made his chest tighten. She was one of the people. That's why everyone loved her—and followed her. She didn't think she was any better—more fortunate, maybe, but no better.

"I'll be damned!" Lou said aloud. "I'll be damned."

"Excuse me?" Yusuf said.

Lou shook his head. "I just fired the one person in my company who leveled with everyone. She treated each person the same. Drove me crazy sometimes, the attention she would give to some of the staff—even the temps." He paused. "I even caught her helping the janitorial staff clean the cafeteria one day when they were shorthanded. I couldn't believe it. Thought she was wasting her time and my money. But they loved her for it.

"Always made a point of parking at the far end of the lot too. Claimed she needed the exercise." Lou gave a heavy laugh.

"And now I'm left with a lot of people like me. People who think they deserve the best." He sighed and looked at Carol, who placed a hand on his back. "I've had the choice parking spot for years, and the choice everything else for that matter, and look what it's gotten me. Since I fired Kate and the others, we've been in crisis. Labor has me over a barrel, everyone's worried, our production is down, our customers are wondering what's going on. And here I sit in Arizona—partly because I need to be here and partly because I don't have a clue what to do about the mess back home. And now it comes to me: I'm the mess. That's what you're saying here—that *I'm* the mess."

"Well, actually, you're the one saying that," Yusuf said. "I didn't say that."

"That's okay, I'll say it," Elizabeth said, smiling at Lou.

But he was somewhere else now. "No wonder everyone loved and followed Kate. Damn. I screwed up."

"So what are you going to do about it?" Yusuf asked.

"I don't know." Lou's voice was sincere.

"Perhaps Kate can give you a suggestion," Yusuf said.

"But I fired her. She's no longer with me."

"On the contrary, Lou, she's never been bigger in your mind than she is now. You might have let her go from your company, but you haven't been able to let her go from your mind. Am I wrong?"

"No, that's about right."

"There is a reason Kate was beloved," Yusuf said. "A reason people followed her and worked for her. And from what I've heard about Kate, I think I know what it was."

"What?"

"Something that one of our Kates—Mei Li—just taught us. Kate created a space for people at Zagrum that was similar to the space Mei Li helped to create for Jenny. I'm betting that when Kate showed up for work each morning, she took off her shoes—metaphorically. In an environment that is often fearful and ego driven, she created a space where people could give up their worries and thrive."

Yusuf waited as Lou pondered this.

"Am I right?" he asked.

Lou still had a faraway look. "Yeah, you might be onto something."

## 18 • SURRENDER

"I know that look," Yusuf said. "It's how I look when I have no real conviction that things can ever get better. It's the look of despair and surrender."

Lou leaned back with a sigh. "Yeah, something like that."

"That feeling is powerful," Yusuf said. "Seductive even. But it's a lie."

Lou broke out of his thoughts. "How do you mean?"

"Because it's assuming something that isn't true."

"What's that?"

"It's assuming that you're stuck—that you're doomed to continue suffering."

Lou frowned. That was exactly how he felt.

"Just a moment ago, Lou, you said that you were the mess. Not others, but you."

"And that's supposed to make me feel better?"

"No," Yusuf said. "But it should give you hope."

"How so?"

"Because if you are the mess, you can clean it. Improvement doesn't depend on others."

"But what if the mess isn't purely mine? What if the people around me are just as messed up as I am?"

"Then you have a huge problem." Yusuf's laugh startled Lou.

"Tell me about it," Lou said.

"Actually, I'm mostly joking, Lou."

"Mostly," Elizabeth noted with a smile.

"Yes," Yusuf agreed, "mostly. Because even if it's the case that everyone at Zagrum is deeply messed up, it's still a hopeful situation."

"How do you figure?" Lou was focused now.

"Because your despair is being invited by another lie. You're assuming that nothing you can do will change them."

"But that's true," Lou said. "I can't change them."

"You're right."

"Then I don't understand your point."

"That's because you surrendered too early." Yusuf's tone was almost cheerful. "While it's true we can't *make* others change, we can invite them to change. After all, didn't Mei Li help to change Jenny?"

Lou thought about it. "Yes, I suppose she did."

"Because we are each responsible for our blaming, self-justifying boxes, we can each be rid of them." Yusuf was gaining momentum. "And since by getting out of the box we invite the same in others, our emotional experience is not dictated by others the way we believe it is when we're in the box. What's more, when we're out of the box, we can begin inviting others to make the changes they need to make. In fact, that is what the best leaders and parents do. So if you surrender, Lou, you surrender to a lie. Your box will win."

"But—" Lou stopped to gather his thoughts. "How do I fight this box I'm in?"

"The same way Avi fought his and I'm fighting mine."

"How's that exactly?" Lou said.

"I think it might help to hear more of Avi's story," Yusuf said.

Avi made his way to the front of the room. "So," he began, "the Arizona outback in the summer of '78."

The group listened as Avi recounted his initial meeting with Yusuf, their early battles, Avi's anger at everything around him—the heat, the bugs, the trees, the earth.

"But everything began to change for me," Avi said, "during a late-night conversation with Yusuf under a clear, starry sky. We were about two weeks into the program at the time, and I'd barely said a word to anyone. As usual, I set up my sleeping spot away from the group, even though that meant I didn't catch much warmth from the fire. I was lying on my back staring at the stars when I heard Yusuf's voice.

"'You know,' he said to me, 'it's the same night sky we see from Jerusalem.'

"I hesitated. But astronomy is a passion. 'Yeah,' I said. 'The Big Dipper, the Polar Star. I remember my dad teaching me all about them.'

"Yusuf sat down next to me. It might have been the first time I didn't pull away from him.

"He said, 'Tell me about your father, Avi.' Well, I found myself launching into a flood of memories from my childhood: how my dad took me on walks every day from as early as I can remember, how he taught me the history of our people, how he played soccer with me at the park, how he always cooked Saturday breakfast, how I loved to travel with him on his surveying jobs, how he always read to me before I went to bed. It was like a dam broke within me and my memories burst free. All my love for my father, the pain of his loss, and the sadness of no longer having him in my life—all of it felt like a grappling hook tugging at my chest. I wanted to be with my dad again.

"Yusuf just sat there with me and listened. Although he couldn't have known it, he was something of a surrogate for my father that night. If I couldn't be with my father, it was at least helpful to be with *someone* after nearly five years of barricading myself from the world. That night was the beginning of my healing. And I will forever be grateful that it happened at the invitation of an Arab. All the blame I'd heaped upon the Arab people for my father's death somehow became more difficult to maintain when it was an Arab who helped reintroduce me to my father.

"When I awoke the next morning, I willingly joined in with the others and helped with breakfast. This was a first for me. Then we broke camp and began our day's journey through the bush. I remember the morning's hike well because it was the first day on the trail that I allowed myself to enjoy where I was.

"Over the following days, memories of another relationship flooded my mind: Hamish. What a friend he had been! So gracious and loyal and kind. He'd come to me in my moment of loss, knowing how deeply I must be hurting and wanting in some small way to help ease my pain." Avi took a moment to blink away some tears.

"And what did I do? I kicked him out of my life. And as if that wasn't enough, I vilified him—with every hurtful word I knew. I blamed him for my father's death. Him! The kid trying to offer me mercy and love. This young boy stuck between two nations—Arab by birth and Israeli by citizenship. I never thought about how he must've been suffering too. How trapped he must have felt watching his family and his country pitted against each other. He was in need of comfort himself, yet he came to comfort me. And in return for that gift, I gave him pain.

"The weight of what I had done settled on me with each hike. The memories felt like rocks added to my backpack. So on another clear evening some ten days later, I sat down with Yusuf again. This time I told him about my friend Hamish and my heartless turning away. The telling was cathartic; I'd never spoken a word of it to anyone until that moment. I had, of course, spent the recent days replaying the events in my mind, but until I was willing to allow another to see my transgression, I was still holding on to and hiding it. Sharing with Yusuf turned out to be part of the healing."

Carol nodded recognition. She thought of the story she shared with the group yesterday, about coming clean to Lou about her eating disorder.

"Part of the healing, but not all," Avi said. "Telling Yusuf nourished within me the seed that had been looking to take hold and grow: I knew in the telling that it wasn't enough in this case merely to feel sorry. Seeing Hamish as I once again did, I felt the desire and need to reach out to him."

"'What can I do for him?' I asked Yusuf.

"Yusuf asked me if I felt the need to do something for him. And I did. That was what my heart seemed to be telling me.

"I wanted Yusuf to tell me what I should do." Avi smiled and looked over at Yusuf. "But—and I doubt this will surprise you—he turned that question back to me.

"He said, 'It's your life and your friend and your heart, right? I cannot tell you what you need to do. Only you can know that.'

"I really felt at a loss. What could be done?

"Well, Yusuf wasn't a complete lack of help." Avi and Yusuf locked eyes again and laughed. "He told me something so simple, yet it proved invaluable. He said, 'Maybe you should ponder the question as you walk over the coming days.'

"And I did. On the third morning, we came upon a spectacular succulent called a century plant. Its stalk was probably thirty feet tall. The century plant lives fifteen to twenty-five years. However, it shoots up a stalk and flowers only in the last year of its life. The energy it takes to grow the stalk ends up killing the plant. When the stalk falls over, it showers seeds on the ground, giving life to a new generation. The low-lying base of the plant is commonly seen in the deserts of Arizona. But the once-in-a-lifetime nature of the stalk, and its determination to grow skyward from rocky, dry soil, lends it an air of hope. Because of the seeds it cradles, every stalk that rises offers the desert the promise of future life.

"I had learned about the plant since joining the survival course and had seen various specimens over the first few weeks. This time, however, when I happened upon one in full flower, something hit me: I had received the gift of a once-in-a-lifetime friend—a friend and friendship that had flourished despite the difficulty of the environment in which we lived. Yet before it could come of age and shoot its flower skyward as a beacon of hope to the desert, I had hacked at its roots and condemned it to death. Towering before me was a surrogate: this plant was now rising as Hamish and I could have risen had I not deserted him.

"I reached up to the lowest of its branches and snapped off a seed. I wrapped up the seed, symbolic both of what I had killed and what I hoped could come back to life, and placed it in my pocket. That evening, I laid my soul bare in a letter to Hamish, apologizing for my inhumanity toward him and for the pain I had caused. I offered the seed as a symbol both of what we once had and of what I hoped we could recover.

"I didn't know whether Hamish or his family still lived in the same little home, but his house number was my only connection to the life I had once known with him. The weekly mail run arrived in our camp two days later. My letter and the century plant's seed started their journey from the desert soils of Arizona to the deserts of the Middle East, hopefully to find a young Israeli Arab still in good health and retaining a spirit that had not been irretrievably damaged by so much violence."

Avi stopped speaking and drank from his water bottle. The group waited for him to continue.

"So what happened?" Gwyn finally asked. "Did you hear from Hamish?"

"No," he said. "I never heard from him."

The energy in the room seemed to sink. This revelation was not what they expected.

"I'm so sorry," Gwyn said. "Do you know what happened to him?"

"Yes. I have learned since that his family moved about two years after I came to the States. They moved to the north of Israel to a town called Maalot-Tarshiha. But he was killed about five years later. He was among the civilians killed by rocket attacks from Lebanon prior to the Lebanon War of 1982."

"Did he ever receive your letter?" Elizabeth asked.

Avi shook his head. "I don't know. There's no way to know."

"What a pity if he never received it," Carol said.

Avi nodded. "I wonder about it all the time—about the pain I caused him and about whether my letter helped to relieve it in any way."

"But writing the letter helped you," Pettis offered.

"You're right," he said. "Even if the letter didn't reach Hamish, it reached me. That's true. For me it expressed an inward recovery of friendship. Hamish may not have received it, but in writing it I finally received him and began to receive others like him."

"Like Arabs, you mean?" Gwyn said. "Like Yusuf and others?"

"Yes. And Americans and Jews and my family and myself—everyone I had gone to war against. Because every human face includes all others. This means that I spite my own face with every nose I desire to cut off. We separate from each other at our own peril."

# 19 • LOCATING THE PEACE WITHIN

"Lou," Avi said, "a few minutes ago you wanted to know how you can get out of the boxes you find yourself in—out of the blame, the self-justification, the internal warring, the apparent stuckness."

"Yes," Lou said.

"From this story I've just shared, I'd like to highlight for you what I believe were the keys to my being released from the captivity of my own boxes—the getting-out-of-the-box process, as we call it."

Lou sat up at full attention.

"First of all," Avi began, "you need to realize something about the box. Since the box is just a metaphor for how I am in relationship with another person, I can be both in and out of the box at the same time, just in different directions. That is, I can be blaming and justifying toward my wife, for example, and yet be clear-sighted toward Yusuf, or vice versa. Given the hundreds of relationships I have at any given time, even if I am deeply in a box toward one person, I am nearly always out of the box toward someone else."

"Okay," Lou said, wondering why this might be significant.

"Which is why," Avi continued, "we can recognize we are in the box to begin with. When we are noticing we are in the box, it is because we are noticing that we aren't feeling and seeing in one direction like we are in another. We are able to recognize the difference because the difference is within us. Which is to say that we have out-of-the-box places within us—relationships and memories that are not twisted and distorted by blame and self-justification."

"Roger that," Lou said, "but what does that have to do with getting out of the box when we're feeling stuck?"

"Because it means we are not stuck."

"How?"

"Think of that night with Yusuf under the stars," Avi said. "It turns out that I had a wealth of out-of-the-box memories regarding my father. Once I allowed myself to find my way to those memories, a lot of things started to look and feel different."

"But you could have made your way to those memories any time in the prior five years but evidently didn't," Lou said. "What made you do it *that* night?"

"Good question. I've asked myself the same thing many times."

"And?"

"And I think the answer lies in the ideas Mei Li and Mike shared with us—ideas that were embedded in the efforts Yusuf made with me and the others who were in the survival course. Remember how Mei Li talked about the importance of doing everything in her power to make the environment an invitation to peace? That is one of our precepts here. The biggest help in finding my way forward and out of the box was finding an out-of-the-box place, or vantage point, within me. In order to give me the best chance at finding such a vantage point within me, Yusuf helped to create an out-of-the-box place around me."

"And how did he do that?"

"By first being out of the box toward me himself. When he approached me that night under the stars, the conversation never would have gone as it did if I felt the blame of his box over the preceding days. I was like Jenny, and Yusuf was like Mike and Mei Li. I was looking to take offense at slights real and imagined. When real offenses wane, however, it gets harder and harder to keep manufacturing them in your mind. Despite my early resistance toward Yusuf, he didn't resist me back. He helped to create for me, you could say, an out-of-the-box place—a vantage point from where I could ponder my life in a new way free from the blame and self-justification of the box. Suddenly, I was free to remember a past that my blaming self-justification had kept me from remembering. I was free to see a different past along with a different present and future. I was freed from the limitations and distortions of the box."

"So what is the getting-out-of-the-box process you alluded to earlier?" Lou asked.

"I've given you the first two parts." Avi turned to the board and wrote the following:

## RECOVERING CLARITY AND FINDING PEACE
### (FOUR PARTS)

### Getting out of the Box:

**1.** Look for the signs of the box (blame, justification, horribilization, common box styles, etc.).
**2.** Find an out-of-the-box place (out-of-the-box relationships, memories, activities, places, etc.).

"First," Avi said, as he turned from the board, "I should be on the lookout for blame and justification—for signs that I might be in a box. I can be on the lookout for signs of the various common boxes, for example—ways I'm feeling better than or entitled or worse than or anxious to be seen as.

"Then when I feel stuck in the box and desire to get out, I can find an out-of-the-box place—"

Lou cut in. "And that's what you found that night with Yusuf?"

"Yes, and in the memories of my dad that flooded back."

"But what about when I'm not on the trail with Yusuf?" Lou asked. "How can I find an out-of-the-box place when all hell is breaking loose around me?"

Lou wasn't trying to trip Avi up at this point. He simply knew from past experience that whatever he was learning from this would likely be swept away and forgotten at the first sign of difficulty. His lunchtime conversation with John Rencher the day before was exhibit number one. He wanted to find some toeholds for himself—things he could remember and latch onto when he felt the walls of the box rising around him.

"Actually," Avi said, "since we all have out-of-the-box places within us, finding one is not difficult so long as we remember to do it. For example, you might try to identify the people toward whom you are generally and currently out of the box. Names will come to mind, and simply thinking about your experiences with those people can take you to a vantage point from where the world seems different than it did the moment before."

Lou nodded to himself. His oldest child, Mary, had just this kind of impact on Lou. She seemed to calm him simply by her presence. It had been that way between them almost since the day she was born. He remembered playing together on the living room floor for hours on Sunday afternoons. Of course, this was before work had taken over his weekends.

"If you needed to," Avi added, "you might call or go to one of these people just to have a conversation or ask for help with the struggle you're having. Or you might try thinking about the people who have had the greatest influence for good in your life and why."

Lou suddenly found himself thinking about Carol and her steady, devoted influence.

"Very often," Avi said, "simply the memory of those people can take you to a different vantage point.

"Or maybe there was a time," he continued, "when someone treated you kindly—especially when you didn't deserve it."

Lou remembered his father's response when he had dumped their new car into the Hudson. He couldn't think of that night without feeling the love that his father had proved was unconditional. He couldn't be in the box when he remembered that night.

"Such memories can be helpful to me when I find that I am in the box railing against someone I don't think deserves to be treated kindly," Avi said. He hoisted himself up on the table at the front of the room, his legs swinging like a kid's.

"Or maybe there is a particular book or a passage in a book or a painting or piece of music that has a powerful effect on you— something that invites you out of the box. Or maybe an activity or place that does the same. Maybe some location that brings back memories of when all was right. For me, I have discovered that Frank Sinatra music, of all things, invites me to an out-of-the-box place! It has this effect on me, I believe, because I began listening to Ol' Blue Eyes when I used to rock our youngest child, Lydia, to sleep. So for me, Sinatra invites me back to the memories of those times—unencumbered memories that give me the chance to think and feel more clearly in the present.

"This all sounds fairly basic, but most people who are trying to find their way out of conflict and bitterness never think to do it. Finding themselves stuck in bitterness, it never occurs to them that they have access to sweet places in every moment.

"Once we find our way to such a place, we are ready for the next step in the getting-out-of-the-box process." Avi hopped off the table and added a third item to the board.

## RECOVERING CLARITY AND FINDING PEACE
### (FOUR PARTS)

### Getting out of the Box:

**1.** Look for the signs of the box (blame, justification, horribilization, common box styles, etc.).
**2.** Find an out-of-the-box place (out-of-the-box relationships, memories, activities, places, etc.).
**3.** Ponder the situation anew (i.e., from this out-of-the-box perspective).

"How do you mean 'ponder anew'?" Pettis asked.

"Could I speak to that, Avi?" Yusuf said.

"Of course. I'll catch my breath."

Yusuf came up to the front. "Pondering the situation anew simply means that once you find an out-of-the-box vantage point, you are now in a position to think new thoughts about situations that have troubled you. Because you will be thinking about them from a new perspective, you'll be able to access thoughts and ideas that may have eluded you while you were trying to think about the situation from within the box.

Yusuf nodded toward Avi. "Avi found that kind of perspective under a star-filled sky. This may not be an out-of-the-box place for you, but Avi's point is that something will be. You need only to identify the relationships, places, memories, activities, and so on, that have that kind of power for you and then remember to search them out when you feel war rising within you. When you've accessed such a place—an internal vantage point where peace remains—you can begin to ponder your challenges anew."

"How does that work?" Pettis asked.

"You learn to ask the right questions."

# 20 • LETTING GO

"Avi shared his story of coming to the States," Yusuf said. "So perhaps it is time I shared mine."

"As you'll recall from yesterday, I ended up in Jerusalem after the city was divided. I began my hustling of Westerners and, as it turns out, my lessons in English when I was about eight. That would have been around 1951. Unlike Avi, I didn't have any friends from across the ethnic divide. In fact, I spent most of my teenage years dreaming of revenge for the murder of my father. And I didn't have to look far to feed that desire. During this time, nationalism among the Palestinian people was taking on a life of its own.

"In 1957, at the age of fourteen, I joined a youth movement known as the Young Lions for Freedom. This group was an informal offshoot of student unions of Palestinians that began emerging in the region's universities in the 1950s. The younger brothers of these students, longing to attach themselves to the causes of their elders, hatched mirror organizations among their neighborhood clans. Ours was such an organization, patterned after the foremost of the student unions, which was located at Cairo University and headed by an engineering student named Yasir Arafat."

Eyebrows raised at the name.

"Yes, one and the same," Yusuf said.

"I quickly distinguished myself as a leader in the organization," he said. "When I was just sixteen, I was invited to Kuwait to meet with the newly established leaders—Arafat among them—of a movement that called itself Harakat at-Tahrir al-Filistinia, or the Palestinian National Liberation Movement. You've probably heard of it as Fatah—the reverse acronym of its formal name. The organization's goal was to replace the State of Israel in its entirety with a Palestinian State through means of armed revolution."

Yusuf paused. "As you might guess, this was an intoxicating vision for a young man set on revenge. I was in.

"I came back from Kuwait looking forward to Israel's destruction. It was only a matter of time.

"My mother, however, did not share my excitement. She distrusted the messengers that would drop notes by my house at all hours of the night. At first she began intercepting the messages; then she started destroying them. She told me, 'I will not lose first my husband and then my only son too!' She had a longer view of the past and the future. She'd say, 'The answer to the tragedy of Deir Yassin is not simply to swap the identity of the parties. You will not take up arms against the Israelis unless they first take up arms against you!'

"Of course I'd point out that they already had. I'd talk about how they'd joined league with the West, assembling the most powerful arsenal in the region.

"She wouldn't hear of it. She'd say, 'What do you know about arms and politics? You are a child, and as my child, you will not enter into league with these night bandits'—that's what she called the movement's messengers.

"But I wouldn't budge. I was my mother's child but also my father's. And in his name, I needed to fight.

"And so I did. I began to act as the cell leader for Fatah in the greater Jerusalem area. This was heady stuff for a young man. And as it turns out, too heady. In 1962, after I had built a grassroots network of over 5,000 committed and loyal volunteer soldiers, or *fedayeen,* a nephew of Arafat moved in and took over the region. I was officially placed as second in command. Everyone in the organization knew the truth, however: I had been stripped of my power."

Yusuf took a sip of his tea. "This was humiliating to me, but my hatred for the Zionist Jews outstripped the humiliation, and I stayed on as a loyal foot soldier. I looked forward to our victory even in my diminished role.

"The apparent final push to victory began in the spring of 1967. In mid-May, Egypt mobilized 100,000 soldiers along Israel's southwestern border and declared that the Straits of Tiran would be closed to ships bound to and from Israel. President Nasser of Egypt then announced his intention to destroy Israel.

"A kind of hysteria took over the Arab world. Change felt within reach. Arab forces from around the region were mobilized on all sides so that by the end of May, Israel was surrounded by an Arab legion force of some 250,000 troops, 2,000 tanks, and 700 military aircraft. I joined a battalion that had taken up a strategic position at Latrun, one of the westernmost locations in the Jordanian-occupied West Bank."

Lou was familiar with this history, but it felt different hearing it in this context, from this perspective. Habit told him to refresh his coffee, but he settled back in his seat. He didn't need caffeine.

"Latrun was located on the highway between Tel Aviv and Jerusalem, the main artery in Israel. It overlooked the Jerusalem corridor, a stretch of Israeli-controlled land that fingered its way to the western parts of Jerusalem but was surrounded by Jordanian forces on the ridges to the north and the south. Latrun would be a key position from which the corridor would be first cut off from the rest of Israel and then captured. It would also be the focal point of the Arab legion's move down the foothills and across the coastal plains to Tel Aviv. I wanted to be part of the eradication of Israel's heart—both Israeli-controlled West Jerusalem and Tel Aviv. There was no better place than Latrun."

Yusuf looked around the room. "But you perhaps know what happened. Avi alluded to it earlier. On the morning of June 5, 1967, Israel launched a surprise preemptive strike against Egypt's planes and airfields, decimating them in a rout. They soon took out Jordanian and Syrian airpower as well, leaving us without protection from the air. We received the command to break into Israeli territory shortly thereafter. But our supply routes were quickly cut off, and the mountains that had been our protection to the east now made our escape impossible. Before night fell, we knew we had been beaten. Jordan agreed to a cease-fire two days later, and the war ended in Israel's total victory just six days after it had begun. When I returned home, East Jerusalem was controlled by Israel. Jordan had been pushed back to the east of the River Jordan; Israel had captured all of Jerusalem and the entire West Bank.

"What followed was a crisis of confidence in the Arab world. A bitter despair swept through the Palestinian people as the Jordanians pulled back within their borders. We were left behind with those we viewed as our captors. We had been abandoned and imprisoned yet again.

"The Fatah network scrambled to regain its footing under the new reality, but we had lost our confidence. And much of our hope. Whatever battles lay ahead, I knew they would be much longer than I had hoped. Regardless, I was not to have a leading role in them. So I started looking for other battles. Battles that could give me release from the daily reminder of our failure as a people and from the gnawing hate I was beginning to carry toward my own—who had, after all, removed me from power and squandered our great opportunity."

Yusuf went to sip his tea, but the cup was empty. He let the story sit in the air.

"So where did you look for a fight?" Pettis asked.

"At first I looked to other Arab nations—to Egypt, to Syria, to Iraq. I looked for some pro-Arab cause that I could attach myself to. Something with promise. Something to give me some kind of hope against Israel."

"So your heart was at war," Lou said. "You were in the box."

Yusuf looked at him and smiled. "Yes, Lou, I certainly was. In a box likely larger and darker than any of you have ever been tempted to enter."

"Careful now," Lou warned. "I have a better-than box. Don't go trying to make your box bigger than mine."

Everyone in the room chuckled at this.

"Did you find what you were looking for?" Elizabeth asked. "Did you find a battle to take up elsewhere in the Arab world?"

"I found battles everywhere," Yusuf answered. "But none worth taking up. They were internal battles for the most part. Everyone was maneuvering to capture power within the vacuum created by the devastation of the war. I wasn't a player in those battles anymore, and their prospects seemed too bleak anyway."

"So what brought you to the States?" Pettis asked.

"Assassinations," Yusuf answered.

"Assassinations?"

"Yes—of John F. Kennedy in 1963 and Malcolm X in 1965. Their deaths made big headlines in the Arab world. The United States was not yet an ally of Israel, and we Arabs looked to America with a bit of hope. I identified with the struggle of Black Americans. Malcolm X, as a fellow believer in the Koran, intrigued me, and I knew a little about Martin Luther King. I was interested in the revolution that seemed to be taking place in America. With my own revolution in shambles, I began looking to the West. Less than a month after the war, I was making plans to go to the United States. I wanted to go to Harvard or Yale to get a degree."

"Ah," Carl said, "that better-than box of yours again."

Yusuf laughed. "Maybe so. On the other hand, they were the only American university names I really knew. A month later, having secured my papers, I boarded a plane in Amman to London and then on to New York City. To make a long story short, I didn't go to Yale or Harvard. I enrolled at the City College of New York.

"On my first day I found my seat in an Introduction to Philosophy class. As the professor was about to begin, a short girl with red hair appeared at the classroom door. With the help of the professor, she made her way across the room, white cane out in front, feeling her way from the door to an empty desk—which happened to be right next to mine. Right away she smiled at me and told me her name was Maeve. I was stunned by her warmth and friendliness.

I don't remember the lecture, but I remember that first impression. I had never met a stranger who was so open and welcoming. It was such a contrast to the way I felt at that moment, guarded and self-protective and defensive. I was to learn that Maeve was burdened by none of the feelings that felt like a constant knot inside me. As the students filed out of class once the bell rang, Maeve turned and asked where I was from.

"When she learned that I had just immigrated from Jerusalem, she was fascinated. She said, 'Tell me all about what it's like there!'

"Over the days and weeks that followed, we met up after classes and spent hours together talking on the campus lawn. We swapped stories of our growing up. She told me all about her childhood in Ireland, and I shared with her the history I have shared with all of you. I wasn't sure if it was because she was blind, but she listened better than anyone I'd ever met before. Though her eyes were closed, I could see in her face that she could sense my pain and my anger. We also talked about the conflict in Northern Ireland, where Maeve had grown up—a conflict that was still raging like the one in my homeland. I had not known much about that history before meeting Maeve, and I soaked up the details. As an oppressed Palestinian Arab, I felt a kinship with the Irish in their long-standing fight against the British."

A few in the group couldn't help but look over at Elizabeth, half expecting one of her quick historical remarks. But she didn't say anything.

"I had found not only a friend but possibly an ally," Yusuf continued. "Here was the equivalent of my Fatah brothers. The similarities were striking: a conflict that was rooted in land but perhaps more so in religion—the Catholic Irish against the Protestants, with Protestants of Irish descent identifying as British. As I said, I knew very little about this conflict when I met Maeve, and I realized that I was getting only Maeve's perspective, but I can remember my frustration as I tried to get her to commiserate with me and she wouldn't. She shared the history of Northern Ireland and how she saw the conflict but always with a disclaimer: Maeve was quick to admit that her perspective was incomplete. There was so much she didn't know.

"I'd push her. I'd say, 'But you've lived it! These are your people. You know what you've lived through!'

"Her response to me was, 'I know what I've lived through, sure. But I don't know what everyone in Northern Ireland has lived through. And I don't know what every British person has lived through. Every single person involved in this has an inner life that is complex. Everyone has a story, and every person has a conviction based on their experiences. And no one, on either side, thinks they are wrong.'

"One day as I began another rant, she cut me short. 'No more,' she said. 'This isn't making you better.'

"This surprised me. But I was ready with a counterargument. I told her, 'I have to talk about this! I have to process it or it eats me up inside.' Why couldn't she see I was being open and vulnerable?" Yusuf smiled.

"Maeve didn't buy it. She said, "You aren't processing it. You're reliving it and wallowing in it and basking in it. You're bringing it back to life every time we talk.'

"And, like that, Maeve went from friend to enemy. I got defensive and told her, 'How can you possibly understand what this is like?'

"She was silent. And so was I. Maybe I knew I'd crossed a line. It was a few minutes before she spoke. She said, 'You've never asked me about my blindness.'

"And it's true. I hadn't. I thought it would be rude. It was a deliberate decision not to ask and I wanted her to understand that. 'I don't think that it defines you,' I told her. 'I've wanted you to feel like I was blind to your blindness.'"

Yusuf paused. "If I remember right, I was pretty impressed with my own wording."

Lou had to laugh. He knew the feeling.

"But Maeve didn't seem impressed. She said, 'But you're not blind to it. And you shouldn't be! It's a part of me. It affects my life every day. But you are blind too, Yusuf. You are blind in a very real way. I can see that. And this blindness is a part of you and it is defining you. And it's true, I don't understand your experience. But I do understand the choice you are making and how it's eating you from the inside. I made the same choice for a long time.'

"Then she shared a story with me—the experience she had when she was fifteen, living in a town called Dunmurry near Belfast. She said, 'One day I was walking home from school with my friends. We were talking and laughing and playing and not paying attention. We passed a British Army post each day, but on that day a British soldier fired a rubber bullet toward our little group. He said later that he fired the rubber bullet in hopes that we'd all run off home. I spent the next few weeks in a hospital. I remember so clearly the day, lying in the hospital, and Ma and Dad told me that when the gauze was removed, I wouldn't be able to see. The bullet had struck one eye but had affected both eyes, and I likely would never see again.'

"I was stunned," Yusuf said. "After so much time talking about the conflict in Northern Ireland, she had never told me how dramatically her life had been affected by it.

"'Why didn't you tell me?' I asked.

"She said that if we had met a year before, she would have. In fact, it would have been all we talked about. Even then, she was consumed with hatred for this soldier and every other British person.

"'When you become blind,' she told me, 'when you can no longer see—every other sense becomes immediately sharpened, even overwhelming at times.' She talked about how sounds had always felt secondary to sight when she could see, but now, sounds were often chaotic and deafening. Memories became more vivid, and they tortured her at night.

"She told me how she used to think about that soldier all the time. She had never seen his face, but she conjured up the idea of him. And hated him. The depression that followed would land her in bed for days at a time. As hard as her parents tried, they couldn't shake her out of it. This went on for years, she said, until she learned his name.

"I asked her, 'What's his name?'

"'Patrick.'

"'And learning his name made a difference?'

"According to Maeve, not at first. But it seemed to crack the shell of her hatred. He had a name. She'd never thought of him as a person before then—someone with a name. It was just a little bit of light, but it was enough to see how dark everything else had become. For the first time she wanted to be free of that darkness, even if she didn't know how.

"She started asking herself, *What is life like for Patrick? What have these last few years been like for him? What burden does he carry knowing what he's done?* At first she wanted to know the answers to these questions, and immediately she had a sense to write him a letter. She knew she needed to talk to him.

"But then the idea repulsed her. In an instant she went from wanting to communicate with this man and wanting to understand him to feeling like reaching out to him would be the worst thing she could do. And just like that, she couldn't say his name, even to herself. The darkness came back. It seemed to her that if any of *his* burdens mattered, then her pain and everything she'd gone through wouldn't matter anymore. She was the victim. He was the victimizer. If anything, he needed to know how much pain he'd caused her. He was the enemy.

"As Maeve told this story, something became clear to me for the first time. I said to her, 'In a way, you had become your own enemy.'

"'It's true,' she said. 'But at the time, I couldn't see that.'

"'So how did you free yourself?' I asked her.

"'One day,' she said, 'I told my ma everything—everything I was feeling and trying to sort out.'

"Her mother thought for a while and then said, 'Part of you sees him as a person, but there's another part of you that won't let you see him as a person. Do you think that seeing him as a person will somehow excuse him of what he did to you?'

"Maeve knew the answer was yes. But she couldn't admit it. Not even to herself.

"Her mother asked another question: 'Maeve, when you felt you should write him a letter, were you seeing him as a person?'

"'Ma, that was the only time I felt ready to see him as a person.'

"What Maeve's mother said next always stayed with her. And it's always stayed with me. She said, 'I have learned that I can trust what I sense to do when I see others as people. When I don't see people as people, I am not seeing them truthfully. And then anything I sense I should do can't be trusted. Seeing Patrick as a person is to see everything you know and to be honest about what you don't know. You know he made a terrible choice that changed your life. But you also know that there is a lot about him you don't know—things you want to know when he has been real to you. I think that following your sense will help you in part because you know it might help him.'

"Maeve wrote the letter. And she got a response.

"Patrick thanked her for reaching out and he apologized. From the letter, Maeve discovered that the choice he made that day changed him as much as it changed her. He was so grateful to finally be talking to her. Eventually they met in person. Maeve said it was a very important day for her.

"Well, I pounced on that. 'See!' I said. 'You're free because he admitted what he did! He apologized! But that's not my story. No one has ever apologized to me. No one has admitted that they were wrong. My father is dead. Who can I write to? Who will say they are sorry? How am I supposed to be free without that closure?'

"Maeve's response put me in my place again: 'I didn't say that his letter freed me. I didn't get his letter for three months. But I was as free during those three months before I received his response as I have been every month since. His letter didn't free me. My letter did.'

"That day Maeve completely dismantled the assumptions I had taken to be the truth. Her story was the beginning of my journey to be free of the box."

Elizabeth broke the silence that followed. "I think that it might be the beginning of my journey out of the box."

"It's a journey we are all on, Elizabeth." Yusuf looked around the room. "All of us."

"And like Maeve," he continued, "our progress rests on our willingness to find our way to an out-of-the-box place where we can ponder our situations anew. We gain this new perspective by asking a series of questions."

He walked to the board and began to write. "Questions like these:"

---

- What are this person's or group's challenges, trials, burdens, and pains?

- How am I, or some group of which I am a part, adding to these challenges, trials, burdens, and pains?

- In what other ways have I or my group neglected or mistreated this person or group?

- In what ways are my better-than, I-deserve, worse-than, and need-to-be-seen-as boxes obscuring the truth about others and myself and interfering with potential solutions?

- What am I feeling I should do for this person or group? What could I do to help?

Yusuf turned back to the group. "With Maeve's help, I started to ask these questions—questions that helped me to ponder my situation anew. For most of my life I had been consumed with my own challenges, trials, burdens, and pains and with those of my people. I had never thought to consider how the Israeli people might feel burdened as well and how I might have added to the burdens they felt. I never considered how I had mistreated and neglected others. As I began to ask these questions, the world began to change for me. I still saw my sufferings, but I was able to see the sufferings of others as well. And when seen in that light, my sufferings took on new meaning. They gave me a window into the pain that others might be feeling, some of it at my own hand. Since I no longer needed to feel justified, I no longer needed to sustain my own sufferings, and I could lay down my victimhood. I began to have feelings for Israelis that I had never felt before. I discovered new desires; I saw different possibilities—potential solutions to our problems that no one who is invested in the box can afford to see. I began to feel hope where before I felt only anger and despair.

"One quick story, if I might," Yusuf continued. "Honestly, it's a quick one. Stretch if you need to—this won't take longer than a half cup of coffee."

Nobody stood up, but everyone heard Pettis crack his back. "Ready when you are," he said.

"I went home to visit my mother a few years after meeting Maeve," Yusuf began, "and I made a point to visit someone else as well. Mordechai had been on my mind. What had happened to him? Was he still on the streets? Still begging? Still being ignored?

"I walked to the square where we had begged together. I asked merchants if they knew of an old man who begged nearby, describing him as best I could. He probably would have been eighty by then, I figured. No one seemed to know him or have any memory of him.

"Finally I happened upon an old woman, herself a beggar. Her dark leathery skin and deep wrinkles spoke of a lifetime on the street and under the sun.

"'Mordechai Lavon? Yes, I knew him,' she said.

"When I asked if she knew where I might find him, she cackled.

"'You won't,' she said.

"'Why not?'

"'Died years ago. Right over there, 'round that corner.' She pointed across the street at an alleyway. 'Body lay there for three days, the police said. No one knew it until he started to rot. What a stink!' she said, recoiling at the memory. 'He couldn't do much, old Mordechai, but he sure could stink!' And she cackled again.

"I was surprised by how badly the news hurt me. What a lonely life he led. So many burdens, so many pains. And yet surrounded by others so focused only on their own pains that they never noticed his.

"As I turned to leave, the woman called after me. 'Hey, mister. How 'bout some money?'

"I felt my neck stiffen—a resistance to her humanity. It was almost a reflex in me.

"*My, the box has staying power,* I thought. I stopped and took out my wallet. 'What's your name?' I asked.

"'Nahla,' she answered, 'Nahla Mahmuud.'

"I reached in and took out all the bills I was carrying.

"'For Mordechai,' I said, extending the bills to her.

"'Sure.' Her face lit up. 'For Mordechai.'"

By now each person in the room was deep in thought and reflection.

Lou's mind was on three people in particular—Carol, Cory, and Kate. A new desire was growing. He wanted to get to know his son. He felt an urge to begin writing a letter to him, to apologize, to share, to joke—to talk. He would have done so in that moment if he hadn't still been in the class. He resolved to write it that evening and to leave it here at Camp Moriah for the next mail run to the trail.

And Kate. He started addressing her in his mind: *I'm so sorry for what I have done—for not listening, for stepping in and controlling how you ran your team, for my stupidity. What can I do to get you back?* That was what he had to do. He had to win her back. He was resolved.

This thought led him to Carol—the woman whose heart he had "won" and then forgotten so many years before. He reached over and touched her hand. *I will not be forgetting again.* But then he realized how naïve this was. Of course he would. The box has staying power, just like Yusuf said. Lou knew he had much more to say to Carol than what he had managed to say that morning. A few good intentions would not overcome decades of bigheadedness. *Whatever she needs, I'll give her,* he told himself.

*But you won't,* came another voice. *You're going to go home and marry yourself to your work again, and she'll take up her role as convenient housemate and caretaker.*

*No, I can't let that happen! I need to change things with the Mordechais in my life before it's too late.* Lou shook his head. How could he sustain that change?

Yusuf came back to the front with a steaming cup of tea. "The ideas we have been discussing will change everything if you can only find your way to an out-of-the-box place to apply them. Each time you find you're getting stuck, whether at work or in your family, you'll have to find an out-of-the-box place just as we have found one together here, and then you'll have to get curious once more. Your questions about others will break you free from your justifications and blame. For a while you will be able to see and feel clearly and to find a way forward that wasn't visible before. That is what has happened to you here, am I right?"

Most of the group slowly nodded.

"Whether you stay free, however," Yusuf said, "and to what extent you do, will depend on what happens next."

"Which is what?" Lou asked.

"The culminating step in the getting-out-of-the-box process."

# 21 · ACTION

Lou waited as Yusuf sipped his tea.

"Although we can get out of the box by finding an out-of-the-box place and pondering the situation anew," Yusuf began, "in order to stay out and away from the box, we have to execute a strategy. That is, we have to do something."

*Now we're talking,* Lou thought. He appreciated direct action.

"Something only we will know," Yusuf continued, "each of us, individually, when responding to the unique needs of the unique people in each situation."

Lou didn't like that answer at all. "But that can't help me then, can it? I'm sorry, Yusuf, but I need more than that."

"You certainly do, Lou, but what you need most is not something I or anyone else can give you. What you might think is not help enough is actually the only advice that can help at all. Anything else would be a lie."

"Then you need to tell me what you mean. I'm not following."

"Sure. Let me tie it back to some of the stories we have talked about together. Remember how Avi felt the desire to write a letter to Hamish?"

"Yes."

"He then acted on that desire, didn't he?"

Lou nodded.

"And do you remember how I felt the desire to find Mordechai?"

Lou nodded again.

"I then acted on that desire, just as Avi had acted on his, right?"

"Yes," Lou said, still unsure where this was going.

"And Mei Li and Mike not only thought about taking off their shoes, they actually took them off.

"And remember Carol yesterday?" he continued. "She voiced an apology to Miguel in front of the whole group, didn't she?"

Lou nodded and squeezed Carol's hand.

"She didn't only think about it, she actually did it."

Yusuf looked squarely at Lou. "I'm going to venture a guess about you, Lou. Do you mind?"

"Go ahead," Lou said.

"I'm going to guess that while we have been together, you have had a number of desires awaken inside you—things you have felt the desire to do or begin doing for Cory or for Carol or perhaps for someone at work. Am I right?"

"Who told?" Lou laughed, but his eyes didn't.

"Then I want you to look again at the board," Yusuf said. "Once I recover a desire and sense toward people, where am I on this diagram?"

"At the top," Lou answered.

"So, out of the box, right?" Yusuf followed up.

Lou nodded.

"The moment you've recovered a desire to help, you are out of the box toward the person. The question at that point is not how to get out of the box, it is rather how to stay out.

"Looking at the diagram from the top," he continued, "what do you need to do now to stay out of the box?"

# THE CHOICE DIAGRAM

## SENSE/DESIRE

**Help Mordechai by gathering his coins for him**

(I'm seeing Mordechai as a PERSON with needs, cares, worries, and fears that matter, like mine do)

**My Heart Is at Peace**

↓

## CHOICE

↙     ↘

Honor the sense       Betray the sense

↓             ↓

I continue to see Mordechai as a person like myself      I begin to see Mordechai in ways that justify my self-betrayal; he becomes an OBJECT I blame

**My Heart Goes to War**

| VIEW OF MYSELF | VIEW OF MORDECHAI |
|---|---|
| Better than | Competitor |
| A victim (so owed) | No right to be there |
| Bad (but made to be) | Robs me of peace |
| Need to be seen as a good person | Zionist threat |
| | Bigot |
| **FEELINGS** | **VIEW OF WORLD** |
| Angry | Unfair |
| Depressed | Unjust |
| Bitter | Burdensome |
| Justified | Against me |

"Honor the sense," Lou said, his mind turning.

"And who is the only person who will know the sense he must honor?" Yusuf asked.

Lou thought about that for a moment. "I guess only the person who is feeling it."

"Exactly," Yusuf said. "And that is why I cannot tell you the precise thing you need to do. Only you, whose life it is—who knows the offenses, the missed opportunities, the petty unkindnesses, and so on—will know. I couldn't have told Avi that he needed to write a letter to Hamish, for example. Only he could have known that. Likewise, he may not have known enough about my life to suggest that I should seek out Mordechai Lavon. And notice, it is not just the sense of what to do but the *desire* to do it that's at issue. That desire has to come from within." Yusuf looked down at his tea, then back at Lou. "As it already has for you, Lou.

"When we have recovered those sensibilities toward others, we must then act on them. We need to honor the senses we have rather than betray them. If you, Lou, for example, were to betray the senses you are currently feeling toward others, you can be sure you would feel justified. You would then be right back in the box. So the key to staying out of the box once you have found your way out is to do what you're feeling you should do. It is to act on the out-of-the-box senses you are having," Yusuf said while adding this as the final step to the list on the board.

Yusuf added a fourth element to the board.

# RECOVERING CLARITY AND FINDING PEACE
## (FOUR PARTS)

### Getting out of the Box:

**1.** Look for the signs of the box (blame, justification, horribilization, common box styles, etc.).

**2.** Find an out-of-the-box place (out-of-the-box relationships, memories, activities, places, etc.).

**3.** Ponder the situation anew (i.e., from this out-of-the-box perspective).

- What are this person's or group's challenges, trials, burdens, and pains?

- How am I, or some group of which I am a part, adding to these challenges, trials, burdens, and pains?

- In what other ways have I or my group neglected or mistreated this person or group?

- In what ways are my better-than, I-deserve, need-to-be-seen-as, and worse-than boxes obscuring the truth about others and myself and interfering with potential solutions?

- What am I feeling I should do for this person or group? What could I do to help?

### Staying out of the Box:

**4.** Act upon what I have discovered; do what I am feeling I should do.

"This, then," Yusuf said, "is how peace can be recovered inwardly, even when we are surrounded by war. We stay on the lookout for signs of the box. We then find an out-of-the-box place from where we can ponder the situation with more clarity. And then we begin to consider others' burdens instead of just our own. In the course of this, we'll typically see things that we haven't seen before. These insights move us to take certain new actions. In the moment we recover this sense or desire to help, we have found our way out of the box. Whether we stay out and retain a heart at peace will depend on whether we honor that sense or desire."

Lou absorbed this for a moment. "But what about the wars around us? They won't be solved simply by finding peace within, as important as that might be."

Yusuf smiled. "That depends."

"On what?" Lou asked.

"On the nature of the conflict," Yusuf said. "In conflicts simply between you and another, I think you'd be surprised by how fully a solution to the inner war solves the outer war as well." Yusuf walked over and stood by Gwyn's seat. "Think about you and Gwyn, for example, Lou. There were times yesterday when you almost got out of your chairs and started duking it out. But look at you now."

They looked at each other. Lou faked a left hook, and everyone laughed.

"But how about other kinds of conflicts?" Pettis asked. "Conflicts with intense history or conflicts between many people. A single heart at peace won't necessarily solve those."

"You're right, Pettis. It won't. But notice what it *will* do. Being out of the box will allow you to see the situation clearly, without exaggeration or justification. It will position you to begin to exert influence toward peace instead of provocation toward war. So, sure—a heart at peace alone won't solve complex outer problems, but those problems can't begin to be solved without it."

Elizabeth jumped in. "Yesterday you said we would end up with a strategy for helping others to change. I assume changing myself in the way you've shown is the necessary first step. But what then?"

"Then you work to help things go right," Yusuf said.

Elizabeth waited for more.

"This is subtle, deep work." Yusuf paused. "But in short, you do what we have been doing with you. So let's talk about that."

# PART IV

---

## SPREADING PEACE

# 22 · A STRATEGY FOR PEACE

"Do you remember yesterday morning when I drew a pyramid and divided it into two levels?" Yusuf asked. "I called one level 'dealing with things that are going wrong,' and the deeper level 'helping things go right.' Remember?"

Everyone nodded.

"Then you'll remember how we agreed that we normally spend most of our time dealing with things that are going wrong, even though that isn't ideal."

The nods continued.

"I'd like to give you more detail around that pyramid," he said. "It forms a structure that governs everything we do here at Camp Moriah with the youth, with the staff, and with you. It shows not only how to *find* peace but how to *make* it. It shows how to replace conflict with cooperation."

Yusuf turned and drew a pyramid similar to the one he had drawn a day earlier. As before, he divided it between dealing with things that are going wrong and helping things go right. But then he divided it still further into six levels and wrote "Correct" in the top level.

## THE INFLUENCE PYRAMID

Turning back to the group, he said, "When we're trying to effect change in others, whether in a child, in a team at work, or in a region of the world, we are trying to correct them, are we not? We are believing that circumstances would be better if another changed. Right?"

"Yes," they all answered.

"But that's wrong, isn't it?" Ria asked. "Thinking that others need to change is already a problem. Right?"

"Well, do you think it's a problem that you want your boy to change?" Yusuf asked Ria.

She frowned. "No, not really," she said.

"If he doesn't," Miguel grunted, "his life'll be a mess."

Yusuf nodded. "So it isn't as simple as saying that wanting others to change is a problem, is it?"

"I guess not," Ria said, suddenly unsure of her understanding.

"What would be a problem," Yusuf continued, "is to insist that others need to change while being unwilling to consider how we ourselves might need to change too. That would be a problem."

"Right," Pettis agreed, "because you wouldn't be able to invite others to change if you were in that kind of box yourself. You'd only invite them to war with you."

"Yes," Yusuf said. "And for one additional reason as well: to the extent I'm in the box toward others, my beliefs about their need to change might actually be mistaken. Maybe my spouse isn't as unreasonable as I've been thinking, for example. Or maybe I've been overreacting toward my child. Or maybe the other team at work actually has some things right. I won't be able to tell the difference between what changes would be helpful and what changes would simply be helpful to my box until I get out of the box."

Yusuf pressed the cap on his marker with a satisfying click. "As we've discovered together over the last two days, the most important part of helping things go right is getting out of the box ourselves."

Yusuf turned back to the board and wrote, "Get out of the box, obtain a heart at peace" in the lowest level of the pyramid.

"For our purposes here," he said, "this is also the biggest thing that has been going wrong in each of our families. Our hearts have been too often at war toward our children and toward each other. So everything we've done together has been with the purpose of trying to correct that. And everything we've done to invite that change is detailed by these middle levels of the Influence Pyramid."

"But they're blank," Lou objected, only half in jest.

"Let's fill them in by considering an example, Lou." Yusuf tossed the marker into the air and caught it behind his back. Lou laughed as Yusuf gave a little bow. "Okay, let's say, for example, that you needed to change something about yourself."

"Purely hypothetical," Lou cracked. "I understand."

"Of course, purely hypothetical," Yusuf said. "Let's suppose when you came in and sat down yesterday morning that Avi had said to you, 'Lou, you need to get out of the box!' Do you think that would have helped much?"

"Well, I think he did just about say that to me." Lou locked eyes with Avi, who grinned back. "But no, alone that wouldn't have done much good."

"What if when you refused, he punished you? Maybe he could have sent you to another room until you wised up. Or maybe he could have withheld water or refreshment privileges from you. Do you think that would have helped you get out of the box?"

"Uh, no," Lou said matter-of-factly. "Withhold my coffee and there will be war."

"I wouldn't dare," Yusuf said. "So you can see that correction alone rarely gets others to change. It will help if I'm out of the box myself when I'm correcting, but even then it usually isn't enough. So what else might help? The pyramid suggests four categories of action that when combined with a heart at peace create a strong invitation to change and peace.

"The first of these is what we have been doing during much of the last two days: we have been teaching."

Yusuf added "Teach and communicate" to the level below "Correct" on the pyramid.

"It is no help to tell you to get out of the box," Yusuf continued, "if you don't even know what the box is. Likewise, any correction at work will be for naught if the people I am trying to correct lack the information they need to perform their jobs. It's the same in the realm of world events. If a country doesn't clearly and persuasively communicate the reasons for actions it is taking in the world community, it invites resistance to those efforts. Whatever the context, if I am failing in my teaching, my correction will likely fail as well.

"Going deeper," Yusuf said, "it is no good trying to teach if I myself am not listening and learning. We've had some ideas to teach you while we are together, of course, but it wouldn't have helped much if we ignored your issues and questions and simply taught according to our plan."

Yusuf added "Listen and learn" to the next level of the pyramid.

Yusuf turned back to the group. "We've been trying to listen to you all the way along, and to speak to the issues you have been concerned about. Yesterday, I think I must not have been doing that very well. You'll remember that Lou thought I was ducking his questions."

"Actually, I think it was more a case of him ducking your answers," Elizabeth joked.

"Probably so." Lou laughed.

"This attempt to learn from you," Yusuf said, "actually goes back to well before you came here yesterday. Remember how we had you write to us about your children?"

Lou and Carol gave each other a knowing look. Trying to craft the letter about Cory had revealed cracks in their own relationship. It had ended in Carol crying and Lou retreating to make business calls.

"That was as much to learn about you as to learn about them. Avi and I have been thinking about you for months and have tried to organize our teaching in light of what we've learned."

"On the subject of learning," Avi jumped in, "another import-ant function of the learning level of the pyramid is that it keeps reminding us that we might be mistaken in our views and opin-ions. Maybe an objective I've been insisting upon at work is unwise, for example. Or maybe a strategy I've been taking with my child is hurtful. Or maybe the lesson structure we had planned isn't work-ing, and so on. The learning level of the pyramid keeps inviting us toward humility. It reminds us that the person or group we wish would change may not be the only one who needs to change! It continually invites us to hone our views and opinions."

"All of which applies as well to world events," Yusuf said. "How effective will a country's communications be if its leaders are not actively trying to learn about and from the people they are trying to communicate with? If we want change in the Middle East, for example, but remain ignorant about the people there and their thoughts and opinions, how effective will our teaching be? And if we are sure about others' need to change but are unwilling to let what we learn from them inform changes in us as well, how much change are we likely to invite? If we are poor learners, our teach-ing will be ineffective. Failure at one level of the pyramid always undermines success at each of the levels above it."

Yusuf turned to look at the diagram. "Which leaves us with two more levels to consider. What do you suppose might undercut my willingness or ability to learn from others and therefore the effec-tiveness of my teaching?"

No one responded immediately.

"How about this?" he asked, writing "Build the relationship" in the next level of the pyramid.

"What if my relationship with the people who work for me, for example, is poor?" Yusuf asked. "What impact do you think that might have on my ability to learn from them and the effectiveness of my teaching?"

Lou's mind went immediately to John Rencher. It was clear to Lou that his poor personal relationship with Rencher made all of Lou's work with the union more difficult.

"Or how about your relationship with the child you brought to us?" Yusuf said. "Would you say it is strong and healthy?"

The silence around the room answered.

"If not, I would guess that there is much you don't know about your child, much that they have not shared with you. Your learning has been stunted as a result, and your efforts to teach and correct have therefore been undercut as well. Perhaps what you need to do is figure out how to build your relationship with your child. Put their problems aside for a moment. What do they like to do? Could you spend time doing that with them? What actions could you take to help build the relationship?"

Lou thought about how he and Cory had not had a heart-to-heart for years. They used to golf together—that felt like a lifetime ago. He didn't know what Cory wanted in life anymore, what he hoped for, or who he dreamed to be. Lou wasn't even sure how Cory liked to spend his time. He just knew that no son of his was going to have a drug problem! And everything he did to correct Cory only seemed to make things worse. And now he knew at least two reasons why: he had been too sure of himself to bother learning from and about Cory, and he had completely abandoned efforts to build their relationship. Everything between them the last couple of years had revolved around Cory's drug problem. It was the subtext beneath every word between them—spoken and unspoken.

Lou sighed. "That hits it on the head."

"What does?" Yusuf asked.

"This build-the-relationship thing." Lou paused to figure out what he wanted to say. "It's so obvious I should have been spending time trying to build my relationship with Cory, but that thought hasn't even crossed my mind lately. It's like the box has blinded me or something."

"That's not far off," Yusuf said. "Think about it: if I'm sure I'm right, there is little hope of seeing where I'm failing. So I keep trying the same old things—the same lectures, for example, and the same punishments. And I keep getting the same outcomes: others with problems. On the one hand, I hate it, but on the other hand, I get my justification, which is what I most want when I'm in the box. My need for justification blinds me to all kinds of possibilities. Even to the obvious ones."

Lou shook his head. He wanted to say more, but his thoughts felt too crowded.

"What's in the last level?" Pettis asked. "Between 'Build the relationship' and 'Get out of the box'?"

"You are," Yusuf answered. "After a fashion anyway. When we at Camp Moriah are thinking about your children, you occupy the next space. That's because this level of the pyramid is about building relationships with others who have influence with the person or group we are trying to help. You have the biggest influence in your children's lives, so if we want to be a positive influence with your children, we better have strong relationships with you. The pyramid reminds parents of the same thing—that they must build relationships with those who have influence with their children, beginning with their spouse. Or former spouse, for that matter."

"How about with their friends?" Ria asked. "Are you saying we need to build relationships with them?"

Carl jumped in. "I hope that's not what you're saying. I don't want my daughter to have some of her relationships. That's been part of the problem."

"Has your criticism of those friends invited your daughter to pull away?" Yusuf asked.

Carl hesitated. "Not really, no."

"Then you might think about applying the pyramid to your situation," Yusuf said. "Let's take a look at the overall structure."

Looking at Carl, Yusuf continued. "I take it you've been trying to correct your daughter's choice of friends—maybe by talking her friends down, for example, or by limiting her ability to be with them."

## THE INFLUENCE PYRAMID

Carl nodded.

"My guess is that although you've tried to talk with her about this, the communication hasn't gone very well."

Carl laughed. "That's an understatement."

"Well, the pyramid invites us to think deeper," Yusuf said. "The next level deeper invites you to consider how well you have been listening to and learning from your daughter. Do you know what she likes in those friends? Do you know what her interests are and why she has chosen the friends she has? Do you know what struggles she is having? Do you know, for example, how your divorce has affected her?"

This revelation surprised Lou. He hadn't known that Carl and Teri were divorced. He looked at the learning level of the pyramid. *Maybe I don't care enough about others to be curious about them,* he wondered. The thought weighed on him.

"Or going deeper still," Yusuf said, "how strong is your relationship with your daughter? The healthier the relationship, the more likely she would be to consider your opinions about her friends. So ask yourself, have you been spending enough time with her to build the relationship?

"And then, finally, how about your relationships with others who have influence with her? With her mother, for example, and with her friends."

Carl looked down, lost in thought.

"You know," Yusuf said, "I learned something interesting with one of my own boys. He had a friend I didn't like either. Not one bit. I tried all the standard father strategies. I talked badly about the boy, kept my son from seeing him, and so on. That's why I could guess the approach you've taken." Yusuf smiled. "When I was complaining about it to Avi one day, he told me that I should practice what I teach! With that nudge, I began to apply the pyramid to the situation. In my case, my son didn't begin losing interest in his friend until I started inviting the friend over to our house. And by then, I'd actually started to like the kid. I was almost sorry to see him go. Until I got out of the box toward my son, my efforts to separate him from his friends only made him want them more."

Yusuf looked at Carl. "The old saying 'The enemy of my enemy is my friend' is the arithmetic of the box. Subtract the box from that equation and you and your daughter may discover new answers.

"In fact," he continued, looking around at the rest, "we'll all discover new answers. If we apply it, the Influence Pyramid will guide us in all our interactions—in our homes, in our workplaces, and in the world. It will suggest actions to take while keeping our minds and hearts clear. It will help us improve our influence for good in every context, even the most difficult ones."

Yusuf looked back at the diagram. "That is, if we remember to apply the pyramid's important lessons."

# 23 • LESSONS

"What do you mean by lessons, exactly?" Lou asked.

"Well," Yusuf said, "the pyramid illuminates three main lessons—axioms that guide its application in all situations. We've already mentioned the first."

He wrote the following:

## LESSON 1

Most time and effort should be spent at the lower levels of the pyramid.

"Remember: we want to spend most of our time in the levels of the pyramid below correction, which is exactly the opposite of what we normally do. We want to focus on actively helping things go right rather than dealing with things that are going wrong. We want to get out of the box, build relationships, listen and learn, teach and communicate. Where circumstances are such that we choose to engage in correction of some kind—whether by putting a little kid in time-out or by sending war planes into the skies above a country that has attacked us—the lower levels of the pyramid become even more important. Correction is by nature provocational. So where we choose to correct, we need to increase our efforts at the lower levels of the pyramid all the more.

"When we actively live these lower levels of the pyramid, we often discover that we need to spend less time on correction than we have in the past. We also discover that when we need to impose correction, it's more likely to have an impact because our correction will grow out of a different place. It'll no longer seem capricious or arbitrary but feel connected to our deeper efforts to help things go right. Whether at home, at work, or among nations in the world, lesson number one of the Influence Pyramid is that most time and effort should be spent at the lower levels of the pyramid.

"Now for lesson two," Yusuf said.

## LESSON 2

The solution to the problem at one level of the pyramid is almost always below that level of the pyramid.

"This lesson also runs counter to our normal reflex. When our correction isn't working, we normally bear down harder and correct more. And when our teaching is going poorly, we often try to rescue it by talking more and insisting more. That is, we drone on in an attempt to correct the problems we have created by droning on!"

Lou thought of all his "teaching" sessions with Cory.

"If I'm correcting on and on but problems remain," Yusuf said, "that's a clue that the solution to the problem I'm facing won't be found in further correction. Likewise with teaching. And if I listen and learn, even going so far as to revise my opinions, but problems persist, perhaps what I need to do is go out and engage with others personally. Maybe I need to increase my efforts to build relationships both with those I'm dealing with and others who deal with them.

"Mei Li shared with us one of the key ways we build relationships here at Camp Moriah: in all that we do with others, we try to 'take off our shoes' with them. We join them in the limitations they face and hold ourselves to the same requirements. For example, the lunchtime assignment we gave you yesterday—to see everyone during that time as a person—was an assignment Avi and I took up as well. And we pondered the conflicts and boxes in our own lives last night, just like we asked you to do. And just as you've had impressions during our time together of things you need to do for someone, we've also had impressions and will leave today with the same commitment as you: to do what we're feeling we should do to help things go right.

"If I find I have trouble building relationships despite my efforts, this second lesson suggests that a solution won't be found simply by spending more time with others. I might have a problem at the lowest level of the pyramid—in my way of being.

"Which brings us," Yusuf said, "to the pyramid's lowest level and to its third lesson."

## LESSON 3

Ultimately, my effectiveness at each level of the pyramid depends on the deepest level of the pyramid—my way of being.

"I can put all the effort I want into trying to build my relationships," Yusuf said, "but if I'm in the box while I'm doing it, it won't help much. If I'm in the box while I'm trying to learn, I'll end up hearing only what I want to hear. And if I'm in the box while I'm trying to teach, I'll invite resistance in all who listen."

Yusuf looked around at the group. "My effectiveness in everything above the lowest level of the pyramid depends on the lowest level. My question for you is why."

Everyone looked at the pyramid.

"You might try looking at the Way-of-Being Diagram from yesterday," Yusuf said.

Lou was the first to speak up. "Well, I can tell you what I see."

"Please," Yusuf said.

"The Way-of-Being Diagram tells us that almost any outward behavior can be done in either of two ways—with a heart that's at war or a heart that's at peace."

"Great," Yusuf said. "And what does that have to do with the Influence Pyramid?"

"Well, everything above the lowest level of the pyramid is a behavior," Lou answered. "Exactly," Yusuf said. "So anything I do to build relationships, to learn, to teach, or to correct can be done either in the box or out. And as we learned yesterday from the Collusion Diagram, when I act from within the box, I invite resistance. Although there are two ways to invade Jerusalem, only one of those ways invites cooperation. The other sows the seeds of its own failure. So while the pyramid tells us where to look and what kinds of things to do in order to invite change in others, this last lesson reminds us that our efforts in any level of the pyramid can't be faked. The pyramid reminds me that I might be the problem and then gives me hints of how I might become part of a solution. A culture of change can never be created by behavioral strategy alone. Peace—whether at home, at work, or between peoples—is invited only when an intelligent outward strategy is married to a peaceful inward one.

"This is why we've spent most of our time together working to improve ourselves at this deepest level. If we don't get our hearts right, our strategies won't much matter. Once we get our hearts right, however, outward strategies matter a lot. The virtue of the pyramid is that it reminds us of the essential foundation—change in ourselves—while also revealing a behavioral strategy for inviting change in others. It reminds us to get out of the box ourselves at the same time that it tells us how to invite others to get out as well."

As Lou listened, he saw how the pyramid could help him at Zagrum. First of all, he needed Kate back. He hadn't known where to begin, but now he knew that he needed to talk with her—teach her about what he'd discovered about himself and tell her about the changes he was committed to making. It didn't stop there: he had to ask her to help him see where he was still blind. He needed to learn from her, and he finally felt willing. As for the relationship, he wasn't sure he could repair it, given how he'd acted. But he suddenly knew where he had to begin. He had removed a ladder she was using as a prop for her team because he thought it was a stupid idea. Taking the ladder was symbolic of deeper problems, just as Kate had said. As silly as it sounded, he knew he needed to bring her a ladder. He resolved that he'd take it to her home in Litchfield, Connecticut, as soon as he and Carol returned home.

Which brought him to Carol. Lou knew he tended toward better-than and I-deserve boxes and that others often faded away into the scenery as a result. He was scared of getting stuck there again—everything about him, Carol an afterthought. But if he could keep reminding himself to work the lower levels of the pyramid, he'd remember to stay in the middle level of learning from Carol—to wonder about her day, her feelings, her needs. It would also remind him to keep building their relationship—to spend time together doing what she enjoys. He looked at the bottom level of the pyramid. A thought came immediately: Carol was the one who had held their family together, often despite him. If he could keep remembering that, it'd be much harder to start thinking he was somehow superior or more important.

Lou finally had some hope. But the fear lingered. "I don't know, Yusuf," he said. "I'm worried I'm going to blow it."

"Of course you will!" Yusuf laughed. "Of course you're going to blow it. We all will. You're a person, after all, not a machine. If the possibility of failure paralyzes you, you might wonder what box is demanding that you be perfect."

"You're saying I have a need to be perfect?"

"It might be worth considering. Need-to-be-seen-as boxes can have a paralyzing impact."

Lou chuckled.

"What's so funny?" Yusuf asked.

"I keep telling myself I don't really have any need-to-be-seen-as issues, but they keep popping up."

"Most of us justify ourselves in all of the basic ways to one degree or another," Yusuf said. "At least I know I do."

Yusuf looked around at each person. "Regretfully—at least for me," he added with a smile, "our time together is about finished. I appreciate the time and effort you've all devoted to this. You've been pondering your lives in bold ways. I hope you'll be both troubled and hopeful as a result: troubled because you know that the box is always just a choice away but hopeful for the very same reason—because freedom from the box is also just a choice away. A choice that is available to us in every moment.

"Before we go our separate ways today, I'd like to mention one more thing. I want to share with you why we chose to name our program Camp Moriah."

# 24 · PEACE ON MOUNT MORIAH

"As we mentioned earlier," Yusuf began, "Mount Moriah is the hill in Jerusalem that is graced by the Muslim shrine known as the Dome of the Rock. This real estate is no doubt the most religiously revered in the world. It is sacred to the Jews as the site of their two Holy Temples in ancient times and valued by Muslims as one of their holiest shrines. And as we have discussed, Christians have traveled in pilgrimage to this mount since the time of Christ.

"Because of this, that revered piece of land is an outward symbol of both our conflicts and our possibilities. One side may say it's their holy place, set apart for thousands of years. Others may believe it was given to them by God. There seems to be little opportunity for peace in such views. Yet in another way, these passionate beliefs provide the portal to peace.

"Think about it. From within the box, passions, beliefs, and personal needs seem to divide us. When we get out of the box, however, we learn that this has been a lie. Our passions, beliefs, and needs do not need to divide us. They can powerfully unite. It is by *virtue* of our own passions, beliefs, and needs that we can see and understand others'. If we have beliefs we cherish, then we know how important others' beliefs must be to them. And if we have needs, then our own experience equips us to notice the needs of others. To scale Mount Moriah is to ascend a mountain of hope. At least it is if we climb in a way that lifts us to an out-of-the-box summit—a place from where we see not only buildings and homes but people as well.

"And so, a land stands divided. And within that land, a meaning-filled hill stands as a symbol of both the divide and the hope for overcoming it.

"Our homes and workplaces are divided as well. Within each of these circumstances there is a Mount Moriah—outward issues that come to symbolize all of the inner turmoil we're feeling. In one home it might be the dishes." Yusuf smiled at Ria and Miguel. "In another, the finances, and in another, the disciplining of the children. At work, we may come to focus on the title or the status or the level of respect we think we deserve."

Lou raised his hand halfway, admitting guilt.

"We begin to do battle around these issues," Yusuf continued, "and the more we battle, the larger they loom on the landscape until finally our homes and workplaces have mountains so high they create their own weather systems. If you don't believe me, just witness what happens to the climate in a room when parties start doing battle around one of their Mount Moriahs.

"The issue, of course, is not the mountain, whether that mountain is the dishes or the finances or Mount Moriah itself. Beneath each of these lies the real issue: why do our hearts make these mountains our battlegrounds?

"Lasting solutions to our outward conflicts are possible only to the extent that we find real solutions to our inner ones. An uneasy détente may be possible in Israel by focusing only on the surface of things—on economics, for example, or on security. But lasting peace will not be. The same can be said for our homes and workplaces."

"But détente *is* preferable to bloodshed," Gwyn said.

"It certainly is," Yusuf agreed. "But let's not fool ourselves. Cool détente, while preferable today, is still a war waiting for tomorrow. Lasting solutions to the battles in our workplaces, homes, and battlefields will come only as we end the war in our souls. We end that war first by finding and extending our out-of-the-box places. And we help others out of their inner wars by being for them an out-of-the-box place ourselves—the way Maeve was for me, the way Hamish was for Avi, the way Mei Li and Mike were for Jenny, and the way all of you have become for one another. We have begun living the pyramid together, which is why our feelings today are so much more peaceful than they were yesterday morning."

The relaxed faces of the group mirrored Yusuf's point. They seemed to have reached a place of ease and trust. Lou glanced around and thought about how the scene looked unrecognizable from yesterday. Not perfect, but encouraging.

"My friends," Yusuf said, "Avi and I and the team here promise that we will strive to be that kind of place for your children. We will take off our shoes toward them, hoping to create a space that invites them to ponder their lives anew and make inspired changes. We invite you to do the same, whatever that might mean for you."

Lou imagined sixty days in the future, when he would see his boy again—shoeless, he hoped, if he could hold on to what he'd learned until then. In the meantime, he had some letters to write.

"But what if my boy still does drugs?" Miguel asked. "What if this program doesn't fix him?"

"Then he'll be lucky to have a father like you, Miguel, who will strive to love him all the same."

"I mean, that sounds nice. But I don't want my kid shooting heroin."

"No, of course you don't. Which is why you won't stop trying to help him, no matter how long it takes. Even if he doesn't like it."

"Don't misunderstand," Yusuf added. "Despite our best efforts, we may find that some battles are unavoidable. Some around us will still choose war. In those cases we have to remember what we learned from Saladin: that while certain outward battles may need to be fought, we can nevertheless fight them with hearts that are at peace.

"And remember the deeper lesson as well: that the peace you hope for—and the peace the world hopes for—depends most fully not on the peace we seek without but on the peace we establish within.

"Which should bring you hope. It means that however bleak things look on the outside, the peace that starts it all, the peace within, is merely a choice away—a choice each of you has already started making. If we can find our way to peace toward children who have stolen from us, spouses who have mistreated us, soldiers who have blinded us, what mountains are too high for human hearts to scale?"

Yusuf looked appreciatively around the room. "Thank you for being here. For bringing your children to us. For bringing yourselves to us. And for giving yourselves to one another. Despite the differences we have had in this room over these couple of days, we have learned to see each other as people, and that has made all the difference, hasn't it?"

Lou, Carol, Elizabeth, Gwyn, Pettis, Ria, Miguel, Carl, Teri, and Avi all nodded.

"Look at each other," Yusuf invited. "Everyone in this room is a person. As are your children on the trail and your enemies, real and imagined.

"Have the honesty and courage to do what our homes, our workplaces, and our communities most need: to see others as people—even, and perhaps especially, when they are giving you reason not to."

 **We hope you enjoyed reading *The Anatomy of Peace.*** In the pages that follow, we have provided additional resources to help you apply the ideas presented in this book to equity, diversity, inclusion, and belonging efforts in your communities and organizations.

For more robust resources and to access a free Study and Discussion Guide, companion videos, and other complimentary bonus materials, please visit **www.arbinger.com/books.**

---

# APPLYING *THE ANATOMY OF PEACE* TO DIVERSITY, EQUITY, INCLUSION & BELONGING

# WHY MOST DIVERSITY, EQUITY, INCLUSION & BELONGING EFFORTS FAIL

As you have now discovered, the ideas presented in *The Anatomy of Peace* provide a powerful guide to understanding the underlying issues at the heart of the bias and discrimination that infect communities and organizations around the world. A heightened awareness of these long-standing issues is prompting new efforts to address them within organizations of all kinds—from government and law enforcement agencies to corporations and nonprofits. Unfortunately, most of these efforts to change biased, discriminatory behaviors focus on changing behavior alone. Despite good intentions, these efforts are doomed to fail. Why? The reason is embedded in the following question: are bias, discrimination, inequity, and a lack of diversity and inclusion behavior problems or way-of-being problems?

Clearly it is both.

As the parents discovered in the story you have just read, attempting to solve any issue that is rooted in our deeper way of being by prescribing surface-level, behavioral solutions is always a recipe for failure. For this reason, to overcome the challenging societal and organizational issues we face today, organizations must first help people change their way of being—the way they see and regard others. No behavioral prescription can overcome the deeper underlying mindset that drives behavior. Not surprisingly, a study conducted by McKinsey found that organizations that "identify and address pervasive mind-sets at the outset...are four times more likely to succeed in organizational-change efforts than are organizations that overlook this stage" (Nate Boaz and Erica Ariel Fox, "Change Leader, Change Thyself," *McKinsey Quarterly,* March 2014). Nowhere is this more true than in organizational initiatives to address diversity, equity, and inclusion.

To succeed, then, we must first change our mindset—our deeper way of being. The following pages provide practical tools to help you approach these critical issues in a way that invites the real and lasting change our communities and organizations so urgently need.

# ORGANIZATIONAL DIVERSITY ASSESSMENT

Before determining what steps to take to improve diversity, equity, and inclusion, answer the following questions to assess the current state of your organization:

## HOW DIVERSE IS MY ORGANIZATION?

| | |
|---|---|
| Y / N | Is a diversity of race, gender, religion, political persuasion, sexual orientation, and physical ability represented throughout the organization? |
| Y / N | Is this diversity represented at all levels of the organization? |

*If the answer to either of the above questions is no, consider the following possibilities and check any that apply to determine the reasons why:*

☐ The organization is not a place where diversity is welcomed and valued. As a result of our lack of inclusion, candidates do not join our team or elect not to stay.

☐ The organization welcomes diversity but does not value it highly enough yet to proactively recruit diverse candidates.

☐ The organization recruits diverse candidates, but there is not yet equity in our internal development and promotion policies and practices.

☐ Despite the efforts of our organization, an underlying bias is manifest in exclusive, discriminatory, or hostile day-to-day behaviors of individuals across the organization.

# The considerations above illuminate three principles that govern diversity, equity, inclusion, and belonging work:

1. Diversity must be valued for its own sake for an organization to prioritize those things that promote and enable it.

2. Diversity at every level of the organization is a natural byproduct of proactive recruitment of diverse team members, equitable promotion and development, and a culture of belonging characterized by inclusive practices.

3. No systemic changes can overcome the effect of unaddressed bias in the team members who comprise an organization.

# WHERE TO START? NOT WHERE MOST THINK.

Having assessed the current state of your organization, where do you start? It is natural to want to correct everything that is problematic. But think of correction of biased and discriminatory behaviors, practices, policies, and structures as the very top of the Influence Pyramid that you learned about in this book. While our solutions at the correction level might be precisely what is needed and our communication with our employees regarding these changes might alleviate our felt need to do something quickly, this is often not the most helpful place to start. Why? Because to be successful, our efforts to correct these issues—like any correction efforts—must be informed by the deeper levels of the pyramid.

## QUESTIONS FOR ORGANIZATIONAL LEADERS

*Before attempting to correct the problematic behaviors in your organization, ask yourself the following questions. Rate yourself on the 1 to 5 scale provided, where 1 is poor and 5 is excellent:*

| | |
|---|---|
| As an organizational leader, how well do I know what is really going on throughout the organization? | ① ② ③ ④ ⑤ |
| How well do I understand the needs, challenges, and objectives of the people that make up the organization? | ① ② ③ ④ ⑤ |
| How well are their needs represented in the decision-making regarding my organization's policies and practices? | ① ② ③ ④ ⑤ |
| How well do I understand the impact of the structures and policies we create? | ① ② ③ ④ ⑤ |
| How eager are we to discover other ways we create challenges in the organization? | ① ② ③ ④ ⑤ |

# THE HUMANIZING POWER
# OF LISTENING

Once we have assessed our awareness of the real issues that need correction, we can begin the important work of listening and learning. This listening and learning must occur broadly and deeply within an organization prior to initiating organization-wide corrective efforts to teach and communicate.

## THE INFLUENCE PYRAMID

The experience of one corporate director of diversity, equity, inclusion, and belonging illustrates the importance of this step. She related how her organization moved forward to institute a new practice that the leadership team believed would signal a commitment to greater inclusivity. However, they did this without the input of those most affected by the initiative. "Despite the fact that our leadership acted with good intentions, they failed to understand what this initiative would mean for the people that were impacted most," she said. "The mistaken assumptions that influenced some of our misguided actions in the past are the same assumptions we are operating from now as we are devising and implementing our 'solutions' to those very problems. Those who have been marginalized feel no more listened to or involved in decisions that impact them than they were before." They had failed to build the requisite foundation of listening and learning and building relationships.

So listen.

But a word of caution. Beware of the box. It is hard to listen when we're in it. And if we do happen to hear the words others say, we will usually miss their meaning. What is required is listening to learn. Not the kind of listening that sorts what others say (or don't say) through the lens of our justification-seeking agenda. Not the kind of listening that intensely looks for fallacies and logical flaws. Not the kind of listening that pounces on inconsistencies or a poorly chosen word or phrase. Not the kind of listening that waits anxiously for an opening or a segue to what we want to say. And most importantly, not the kind of listening that pays more attention to what is said than what a person is trying to say.

When we are not seeking justification, we recognize that there is more value in understanding meaning than parsing words. And when we see people as people, we seek to find the most charitable way to infer meaning from words, which are always a grossly imperfect medium to convey that meaning.

Is there a more important time for this kind of listening than now, especially with those who are different from us in some way? How interested are we in really understanding others? How eager are we to learn from others the kinds of things that might dispel the discriminatory darkness from those parts of us that are invested in maintaining the justifications we prop up through prejudice, misconceptions, and fear? How eager are we to listen to see ways we can change? What would happen in your organization if everyone felt listened to in this way?

# ASSESSING MY LISTENING

A simple question can help us become more aware of our true motivation in situations that require us to more fully understand others:

*"Am I listening to correct and teach, or am I listening to learn?"*

As you prepare to spend more time doing the work of listening and learning before executing corrective efforts, commit to listening and learning in the following three ways:

- **Listen to learn about the person**
- **Listen to learn from the person**
- **Listen to learn how I may be mistaken**

Listening with these three imperatives in mind creates a deep connection between the listener and the person being listened to. It enables the listener to hear things they haven't heard before. As we listen in these ways, we will begin to deeply understand the many dimensions that make up those we are listening to. We will begin to understand what their experience is like working in the organization and, perhaps most importantly, their experience interacting with us. Unfortunately, listening is often thought of as a burden we impose on ourselves for the benefit of others, as if it were a gift we give to others. But real listening is primarily a gift we offer ourselves—one that opens us up to others and allows us to live and work free of prejudices, biases, and false assumptions.

What's more, this kind of listening will most often lead to a sense of something we can do to help things go right.

Whatever role we play in our organizations, the influence we have in the actions we take will be, in large part, a function of the degree to which we allow ourselves to be influenced by others. And more often than not, this kind of listening helps us see where we can engage in the most important correction of all—the correction of ourselves.

Understood properly, the Influence Pyramid is a structure that is primarily about correcting ourselves and our organization, not others. Whether this involves correcting what we allow and tolerate as an organization or identifying and rooting out our own bias as leaders, everything we do beneath the top level of the pyramid prompts us to consider steps we can take to correct ourselves and our organizations and thereby invite the change we hope to see.

# BUILDING MEANINGFUL RELATIONSHIPS

Not all our efforts to listen and learn will be met with others' willingness to really share the truth about their experience and views. The degree to which others feel safe sharing this with us will be a function of the strength and depth of the relationship we build. Without a relationship, we shouldn't expect that others would share their experience or their views about how we may need to improve and how our organizations might need to change. And even more foundational is the relationship we have with others who influence the person or group of people we want to learn from.

With this in mind, consider the relationships you have with the people on your team—those closest to you in the organization. Ask yourself this question:

*Do my relationships with people who look like me—in skin color, gender, sexual orientation, age, religious views, or physical ability—seem different in quality than those with people who don't look like me in any of these ways?*

This is an important question. It provides an important gauge to help us see the degree to which we see others as people. If we have a different level of relationship with those who look like us versus those who don't, despite the fact that all of them are on our team, we should ask ourselves why.

Thinking about how the pyramid provides more clarity regarding how we see those on our team may prompt us to ask another important question:

*Do I have stronger relationships with those who have influence with the people who look like me versus those who don't? For example, do I know the names of the family members of those who have influence with people who look like me versus those who don't?*

If you have broad influence in your organization, you might invite leaders at every level of the organization to consider these questions in relation to the people who directly report to them. Then have them ask themselves where they may need to build relationships. Once they have evaluated their relationships with others, invite them to ask this final question:

*Do I see the people with whom I have not invested time to build a relationship as people—really?*

To assist team leaders in these efforts we have included a checklist of these and other helpful questions to consider:

## QUESTIONS FOR TEAM LEADERS

*To assist team leaders in these efforts, we have included a list of these and other helpful questions to consider. Rate yourself on the 1-to-5 scale provided, where 1 is poor and 5 is excellent.*

| | |
|---|---|
| How well have I listened to those I lead? | ① ② ③ ④ ⑤ |
| How fully do I understand the aspirations and challenges of those I lead? | ① ② ③ ④ ⑤ |

How well do I understand my impact on those I lead? ① ② ③ ④ ⑤

How well have I listened to and learned from team members who identify as part of a minority group? ① ② ③ ④ ⑤

Do my relationships with people who look like me—in skin color, gender, sexual orientation, age, religious views, or physical ability—seem different in quality than those with people who don't look like me in any of these ways? ① ② ③ ④ ⑤

If someone identifies as a member of a minority group in our organization because of the color of their skin, their physical abilities, their religious convictions, their sexual orientation, their gender, or any other aspect of their identity, do I really know what it is like for them to work on our team and in our organization? ① ② ③ ④ ⑤

Do I have stronger relationships with those who have influence with the people who look like me versus those who don't? For example, do I know the names of the family members of those who have influence with people who look like me versus those who don't? ① ② ③ ④ ⑤

How inclusive is the environment I have created as a leader? Does everyone feel that our team is a place they belong? ① ② ③ ④ ⑤

Have I used my knowledge of the needs of minority team members to improve my own leadership? ① ② ③ ④ ⑤

Have I used my knowledge of the needs of minority team members to influence change in the organization as a whole? ① ② ③ ④ ⑤

It's important to remember that each level of the pyramid above the lowest level is a behavior. The effectiveness of these behaviors is a function of the way of being of those who employ them. Our way of being—how we see others—is the most foundational level of the pyramid.

## THE INFLUENCE PYRAMID

Whether we are leading a team or a family or are in a corporation or city government, we can build relationships only to the degree that we are willing to share our hopes, goals, needs, challenges, objectives, and headaches with others. This is perhaps the most important distinction between the "Build the Relationship" level of the pyramid and the "Listen and Learn" level. We can listen and learn and get curious about others' hopes, goals, needs, challenges, objectives, and headaches only to the degree that we have shared the same with them. This is the basis of any relationship.

Relationships are built on trust, and we invite others to trust us when we trust them enough to really share ourselves with them—to trust them with our experiences, views, worries, and challenges. We should never expect anyone to share anything deeper or more honestly with us than we have shared with them.

# RECOGNIZE POWER DYNAMICS

Part of this endeavor will include recognizing the power dynamics at play within your organization. Where do you find yourself in the chain of decision-making? If you are not in a position to make decisions that would institute broader change in your organization but want to have influence, consider the strength of your relationships with those whom can institute these changes. Find those who you trust in the organization and with whom you feel safe to share your thoughts. Perhaps you are a decision-maker and wonder why no one has spoken out before now. What do you need to change to create a space of safety and inclusion for those who report to you?

# STAY FOCUSED ON PEOPLE

Disciplining ourselves to invest time at the lower levels of the pyramid will ensure that we do not simply overlay antidiscriminatory policies on an organization of people who have not worked to eradicate bias or prejudice from their own hearts. And rather than positional leaders designing for people, when we see others as people we create a new way of working with the people whose experiences and perspectives ought to be at the heart of organizational change. Applying the lessons of the pyramid will help you stay focused on people—to approach diversity, equity, and inclusion efforts in a way that does not only work to eliminate dehumanizing behaviors and practices but transforms the way we see each other. And real change at that level can change the world.

# INDEX

# ABOUT THE ARBINGER INSTITUTE

The Arbinger Institute delivers training, consulting, coaching, and digital tools to help individuals and organizations transform culture; improve diversity, equity, and inclusion (DEI); accelerate collaboration and innovation; and resolve conflict. Employees of organizations that embed Arbinger's way of working experience a fundamental change in mindset that leads to lasting changes in their behavior and in the results they are able to achieve.

Since the institute's inception in 1979, the implementation of Arbinger's work has fueled the success of clients that span every industry. As a result of its over forty-year track record, Arbinger is now recognized as a world leader in the areas of mindset change, culture change, DEI and belonging, leadership development, team building, conflict resolution, and strategy.

Worldwide interest in Arbinger's work has propelled the growth of the institute across the globe. Headquartered in the United States, Arbinger now has offices in nearly thirty countries, including throughout the Americas, Europe, Africa, the Middle East, India, Oceania, and Asia.

Arbinger's first book, *Leadership and Self-Deception,* originally published in 2000, is one of the top fifty bestselling leadership books of all time and introduced Arbinger's work to a global audience. *The Anatomy of Peace,* Arbinger's second book, was published in 2006. Since then it has been printed in nearly thirty languages. Year after year since its original publication, *The Anatomy of Peace* has been one of the topselling conflict-resolution books in the world. Few books in history have performed so strongly in their categories over such a long period. *The Outward Mindset,* first published in 2016, shows how to successfully implement the ideas from *Leadership and Self-Deception* and *The Anatomy of Peace* in organizations. Individually and together, these books help readers see their lives and work situations in entirely new ways and discover practical and powerful solutions to the seemingly unsolvable problems that plague organizations.

The Arbinger Institute's mission is to turn the world outward—to help individuals, teams, and organizations get out of the inward-mindset box and become more connected, aware, and attentive to the needs, objectives, and challenges of colleagues, neighbors, family members, and even rivals. Arbinger works with organizations both large and small, well known and out of the spotlight. Arbinger's clients range from nonprofit organizations and high-tech start-ups to many of the largest companies and governmental institutions in the world.

Sustained growth of our clients cannot come from expertise that resides outside their organizations. While short-term growth sometimes can be achieved in this way, ongoing growth cannot be outsourced. An organization will rise only as far as its own people are equipped to take it. For these reasons, Arbinger positions and equips clients with deep expertise in its tools and processes to be able to "consult themselves" over time.

Arbinger often embeds its expertise within client organizations by preparing and certifying their employees to deliver Arbinger's programs within their organizations. To learn more about Arbinger's training, consulting, coaching, and digital tools, to find out how to become an Arbinger facilitator within your organization, or to explore other Arbinger publications and access client case studies, please visit arbinger.com or contact us by phone at our US headquarters at 801-447-9244.

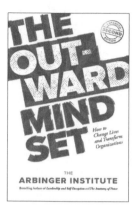

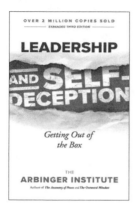

**Berrett–Koehler**
Publishers

**Berrett-Koehler** is an independent publisher dedicated to an ambitious mission: *Connecting people and ideas to create a world that works for all.*

Our publications span many formats, including print, digital, audio, and video. We also offer online resources, training, and gatherings. And we will continue expanding our products and services to advance our mission.

We believe that the solutions to the world's problems will come from all of us, working at all levels: in our society, in our organizations, and in our own lives. Our publications and resources offer pathways to creating a more just, equitable, and sustainable society. They help people make their organizations more humane, democratic, diverse, and effective (and we don't think there's any contradiction there). And they guide people in creating positive change in their own lives and aligning their personal practices with their aspirations for a better world.

And we strive to practice what we preach through what we call "The BK Way." At the core of this approach is *stewardship,* a deep sense of responsibility to administer the company for the benefit of all of our stakeholder groups, including authors, customers, employees, investors, service providers, sales partners, and the communities and environment around us. Everything we do is built around stewardship and our other core values of quality, partnership, inclusion, and *sustainability.*

This is why Berrett-Koehler is the first book publishing company to be both a B Corporation (a rigorous certification) and a benefit corporation (a for-profit legal status), which together require us to adhere to the highest standards for corporate, social, and environmental performance. And it is why we have instituted many pioneering practices (which you can learn about at www.bkconnection.com), including the Berrett-Koehler Constitution, the Bill of Rights and Responsibilities for BK Authors, and our unique Author Days.

We are grateful to our readers, authors, and other friends who are supporting our mission. We ask you to share with us examples of how BK publications and resources are making a difference in your lives, organizations, and communities at www.bkconnection.com/impact.

Dear reader,

Thank you for picking up this book and welcome to the worldwide BK community! You're joining a special group of people who have come together to create positive change in their lives, organizations, and communities.

## What's BK all about?

Our mission is to connect people and ideas to create a world that works for all.

Why? Our communities, organizations, and lives get bogged down by old paradigms of self-interest, exclusion, hierarchy, and privilege. But we believe that can change. That's why we seek the leading experts on these challenges—and share their actionable ideas with you.

## A welcome gift

To help you get started, we'd like to offer you a **free copy** of one of our bestselling ebooks:

### www.bkconnection.com/welcome

When you claim your **free ebook**, you'll also be subscribed to our blog.

## Our freshest insights

Access the best new tools and ideas for leaders at all levels on our blog at ideas.bkconnection.com.

Sincerely,

Your friends at Berrett-Koehler